The Prison Letters
Apostle Paul's Letters To The Early Church

Written and illustrated by Jeff Todd

The Prison Letters:
Apostle Paul's Letters To The Early Church

Published by:
Jeff Todd
Newnan, Georgia

ISBN-13: 979-8-3304-9418-7

The purpose of this book is to share the Good News of Jesus Christ and put it out there in an easy-to-understand way. It is part of the outreach ministry of Jeff Todd.

Please note that there will be mistakes and misprints in this book. We are all human, right? We hope you won't find too many of them. This book was edited to the best of the author's ability and he will not be held responsible for errors.

Direct all correspondence to:

A BackPew Review
c/o Jeff Todd
PO Box 71972
Newnan, GA 30271-1972

Contents

Contents

Introduction – 5

More from A Berkrew Review – 391

Introduction
By Lewis – The Common Tater

Reading the Bible freaks a lot of people out. Many feel that it's too complicated and should only be read by preachers or teachers and then translated so that they can understand it. Nope! That's the wrong way to look at it.

The fact is God's Word is for everybody. Anyone is able to make sense of it because God makes it possible through His Holy Spirit living within us. He will reveal spiritual things that apply to our life. For many of us, its just a matter of taking the time to open it up and read it.

If you knew that everything you needed to know about how to live life successfully was in there, wouldn't you want to read it for yourself? We also live in an age where people are listening to false doctrine and don't even know it. We don't take the time to compare what we are being told by preachers with what God's Word actually says. Many folks are being led astray. It's important to know the Truth! Try and think of the Bible as God's Words spoken directly to you on a personal level.

Since you have a copy of this book in your hand, you're probably wondering what it's all about. What's A BackPew Review? Right? If I had to give a quick answer, it's basically a simple man's perspective of what he receives from reading the Bible.

You see, I am an average ordinary person, just like you, that wants to live the Christian life the best way I can and hear what God is saying to me through His Word. I am basically writing down my thoughts from what I learn from the Bible and through life in general. I have no worldly qualifications, certifications or doctrinations that makes me the man for the job. I am a simple person – a nobody in the eyes of the world. However, I am saved and that makes me a child of God. And that's cool!

I also take the Great Commission seriously. Jesus told the disciples long ago to share the Gospel and take it to the four corners of the world. I feel that assignment was meant for us as well. Each one of us has a responsibility to let others know about Salvation – what it is and how to get it - and to tell someone what Jesus did for them on the cross.

For many of us, the questions are how do we do it and when can I get started? Right?

For me, I have to use what the Lord has given me. This includes the relationship I have with Jesus, His Word, and the gifts, talents, and characteristics that He molded into me from the day I was born. This also includes my ability to draw and write. Your gifts may be different, but are very important to God and should be used right away. And since Jesus is returning soon, the time you should begin sharing the Gospel is now.

I don't want you to get the wrong impression. The purpose of this book is not to be a substitute for reading the Bible. I feel everyone should read it. I don't want you to think I am poking fun at God's Word or trying to offend any religion. That's not my purpose. My hope and intentions for writing this book is that it will inspire you, as the reader, and will offer humorous illustrations to use in your walk with Christ. I want to present the Bible out there in a simple and easy-to-understand way so that everyone can get it. We can learn together how to live our life to its fullest with happiness and joy that God intended for us to live.

Hopefully, by reading this book, you'll see that being a Christian doesn't have to be boring and dull. I believe it should be energetic and alive like wired-up kids on a sugar high. We are to be a light in the world that we live in and shine out to others. When a person sees the way we are, it should make them want to be that way, too. Our lifestyle should point them to Jesus. Everything we say and do should reflect the One that saved us.

I have never considered myself to be like everyone else. The way I look at life may be different than the way others see it. Even as a young child, Christian people to me were always so serious and stiff-necked. It was almost like they were afraid to smile. I agree, it was wrong of me to segregate Christians like this, but those were the Christians I knew. As I grew older, I realized that some Christians were actually normal people and reflected Jesus in the way they acted.

I know from personal experience that being a Christian isn't hard. It's not a series of rituals or following a magic formula. It's actually so simple that anyone can be one. However, walking the Christian walk can be difficult and requires understanding of God's Word and applying it to our life. That's my purpose and focus of writing this book! I want to write something that would minister to people (no matter who they were) and possibly help them understand what it means to be a Christian and share with them the Gospel that leads them to eternal life.

It's got to be simple and easy to understand. I don't use BIG words when I speak, so I will not write BIG words when I am using this to reach people and lead them to Jesus. I can't! It's not how God made me! If you're reading this today, this book is for you from a simple-minded person like me. Being a Christian is awesome and it's not as weird as you may have heard. We're not crazy people! But, I am on a mission to show people how they can be saved.

One of the most important decisions we'll ever make is turning from our sinful nature and asking God for forgiveness. If you have never asked Jesus to come into your life, I hope and pray that you make that choice today.

Excuse me for a moment. I want to pray for you and for God's blessings on this book.

Dear Lord, I pray right now that You use these words from this book to reach people out there. Only You know who this is intended for and who will be reading this. I ask that you use it for Your glory and that this book will lead them to You. I give You all the praise and honor, Lord. Thank You for all that You do for me, Jesus. Amen.

This book is my personal commentary. I am sure there are several books floating out there and sermons preached around the world on the same thing, but this is what I received from doing my own personal study. It's a simple read.

If you find words that aren't spelled right, I'm sorry. If there are words left out, I apologize. This is about as good as it's going to get. I hope it is a blessing to you anyway and that you receive something from it.

So, here it is folks!

The Prison Letters
Apostle Paul's Letters To The Early Church

The Book Of
Romans

The Book of Romans

Introduction to the Book of Romans

I enjoy reading God's Word. It's full of wisdom and spiritual information that just puts our life into perspective. It gives us a focus that points us in the direction of Jesus Christ. And that's cool!

Many people make the Bible too complicated. Some take the words and twist it to suit their agenda. Some take sections of it and add it to other sections and with a mental piece of duct tape, they create something that means something totally different than what those scriptures originally meant. The Bible's not complicated at all and is actually simple to understand. I would advise praying before you read it first and allow the Holy Spirit to guide you in it.

Today I begin a study on the Book of Romans. You've heard of it, right? It's the book right after Acts. You may have heard of the Roman's Road, which are scriptures from Romans that share the path to receive one's salvation. That's why it's called a road. Anyway, we'll be reading them again in this book.

Before we begin, here are some cool facts you should know that will give us a jump start before we dive into it. Romans was written by the Apostle Paul around A.D. 57 to the Christians living in Rome during that time. Paul was hanging out in Corinth and wanted to introduce himself to them and share with them a sample of his message before he arrived there. It was a letter, but it didn't really have the characteristics of one. Paul used it to present a statement of his faith.

If you would, grab your Bible and read along with me. I'll include the verses so that it will make it easier for you to follow along. There are sixteen chapters and we'll study each one and see what God has in there for us. As with other books from the Bible, I'm sure it's going to be some good stuff.

Paul's Introduction
Romans 1: 1-7

As we already know, Paul was a Christian. He considered himself a servant of Jesus Christ, but he wasn't always one. Oh no! Before he was saved, he was a Christian slayer and that means literally what it says. He killed Christians. Completely different than what he was as he was writing Romans. He was a bad dude, but something cool happened on a road he was on heading to Damascus and his life was changed forever. He saw the Light! And instead of acting like a deer when it sees headlights, Paul took off running.

In these verses, Paul is addressing the Christians in Rome. He was telling them who he was and who he now serves. He tells them about Jesus Christ and shares a brief detail of the Good News. Good News? Yes. Jesus, the Son of God, was born in human form as a descendant of King David, His death and resurrection, and His grace and salvation that He freely offers anyone and everyone. That was almost hard to say in one breath, but that's what he was telling them about.

WHAT WAS PAUL DOING BEFORE HE BECAME AN AWESOME WRITER? WELL, LET'S JUST SAY... IT DIDN'T INVOLVE A PEN.

And the obedience that comes from faith? Well, there's just something about being a Christian that makes you want to tell others about your experience and all the cool things God has done for you. It also makes you want to serve Him in whatever area in life He places you in. It could be anything. You could be a preacher or a proud member of the custodial staff. It doesn't really matter, you just want to serve. Right?

Obedience is surrendering and doing what the Lord wants you to do. Are you doing it? If not, why not? It could be as simple as sharing what you got in Jesus with someone you know. Tell somebody.

Paul's Longing To Visit
Romans 1: 8-17

You could tell Paul was getting excited by writing these folks. He

had heard that many of the Romans were saved. Paul was a Roman himself and hearing this news would be like hearing that your family became Christians while you were on vacation for a few years. Wouldn't that be awesome? It would be exciting because you had been praying for them while you were gone and now their life had been changed for the good. I would be excited too and couldn't wait to get back home.

Paul tells them that he is not ashamed of the gospel for the simple fact that there is power in it and he had seen it for himself. Throughout his journeys where he preached it, he saw miraculous things happen. He couldn't wait to share it with them in person.

Have you ever had an experience with God? It could be where you prayed about something and applied one of God's promises from His Word. One day God answered your prayer and the thing you prayed for happened. Pretty amazing wasn't it? I bet you told somebody, didn't you? That's how it is. God's miracles get an audience, whether they see it first hand or someone tells them about it.

The more we surrender ourselves to God the more He presents Himself to us. We begin living more in the spiritual realm and become closer to Him. This type of faith develops righteousness. God's all about us being righteous and we should make it a point to live like it and that means living by faith.

God's Wrath Against Mankind
Romans 1: 18-32

People want to think that God is all about love and He is, but He also has a violent side of Him that's against sin. We kid ourselves into thinking we can live our life how we want to without worrying about the guilt we have for doing it and knowing that God is against it. People naturally know what is right and what is wrong. The Bible says that God has made it plain to everyone. People know it! The problem is that the world has turned its back on God. For that reason, God's wrath will be poured out on mankind. That might be a side of God that you may not have wanted to know. The reason He hasn't done something about it yet is because instead He has given them over to their own sinful desires, shameful lusts, and depraved mind. The full wrath will come when Jesus returns. I hope and pray that many have changed their evil ways by then. Don't you?

These verses give examples of sin that God doesn't like. Sadly, we see this in the world today and treat it as normal stuff to do throughout the week. Many people reading this will probably be offended, but I can only present what it says in the Bible:

Sexual impurity
Sex before marriage? A black book list of 'booty calls'? Weird sex? I would assume anything that goes against God's plan for marriage. It's not good!

The world has made it seem like sex is just something you do, and when you do it, do it often, and just make sure you wear protection. Right? Ask any fifth grader! Chances are, they probably have 'protection' stuck in their wallet somewhere. Sex was meant to be an act of love and it's a spiritual thing between a man and a woman that made a vow to God to stay together. That's how it was supposed to be. And personally from experience, sex is better when it's done God's way. Just sayin'.

Worshiping and serving created things
Money and material wealth has been in this category for many years, but as many have learned, it will let us down. Anything we put before God in priority in our life could be considered a created thing we serve and worship. The key is for us to check our priorities. What is it that's keeping you from being 'souled-out' to Jesus?

Lesbianism/Homosexuality
Our culture has made this popular and a normal part of society,

but God hasn't. The world has become desensitized on this topic and is making it acceptable, but God doesn't. It's plain and simple from God's Word that this ain't cool. Instead of coming out of the closet, people need to step out of it completely and follow what God is telling them.

Greed
Always wanting more and a little is not enough. It seems our world is all about getting more stuff and it doesn't matter who we hurt to get it. Many companies are guilty of this and lately they have been paying the price. We have to learn to be satisfied with what we have. The big word for that is 'contentment' and if we need or want more, just ask God for it. It says He knows the desires of our heart. Heard that before?

Depravity (lack of morals)
Take a look around you in the world today. Would you say that the morality in society has improved over the past 50 years? Or has it gotten worse? Yes, that's what I think, too. The world is going downhill quicker than a three year old with a wheelbarrow full of bricks...on Mount Everest. That was a good one wasn't it?

The problem is that many people are taking God out of everyday living. People need to know Him and follow His perfect plans. Society has this attitude that they are the ones in charge. They better wake up! A society without God will soon find out why He is needed in it, especially when they're covered in its rubble.

Envy
This is when you want what someone else has. It's not always their personal possessions or money. It could also be wanting to be or act like them. And God ain't all about that! Here's why. He made you to be you. If He wanted you to be like your neighbor, He would have allowed their mother to give birth to you and

made you twins. But He didn't!

You have special qualities that make you unique for the sole purpose of serving Him with. Your special gifts and talents are what you will be working with to do it. Just know that God supplies everything we need to do His perfect work. And if you are envious of other people's possessions, ask God for them instead. He will either answer Yes, No, or Not Yet. Leave all that up to Him.

Murder

Thou shalt not kill. Ever heard that before? That's one of them Ten Commandments. It's a 'No No'. But, if you'll look around, you'll quickly see that someone gets murdered every day somewhere in the world. It's all messed up!

Anger usually sparks the fire that causes someone to kill somebody. To be honest, what this world needs is love. And guess what? God is love! It says so in the Bible. If we spent more time figuring out how to express love to one another, the word 'murder' wouldn't be in our dictionaries or in people's minds for that matter.

The hippies from the 70's almost had it right with the 'Make Love Not War' slogan, but they forgot about sexual impurity. What we really need is God.

Deceit

When people lie to others with the intent to get them to believe something false is considered an act of deceit. The key here is an attempt to get someone to believe in the wrong things.

A salesman or company trying to sell a product to you may tell you that it's the best thing since sliced bread. Even though it's really no better than the same product someone else is trying to sell to you. They twist a few things or focus on one particular thing it offers and lie to make it bigger than it actually is. That's a good example of deceit.

Another example would be these energy drinks that are sold in local convenience stores. The reality is that you basically have flavored water mixed with some stuff in it that nobody really knows what it is and they pump it full of caffeine. They charge you $2 for it. But what you really have is a cup of flavored coffee that you can make at home for about ten cents. But, because the whole 'energy' thing is so sociably cool these days, people will buy it.

The same is true in the bottled water craze that started a few years ago. They marketed this idea that water in a bottle for a dollar is good for your health. It's naturally purified and comes from some exotic stream somewhere. But, if you take a trip to where it's bottled, you would see the same setup as your kitchen faucet. Basically, they made money off of something you can get for free.

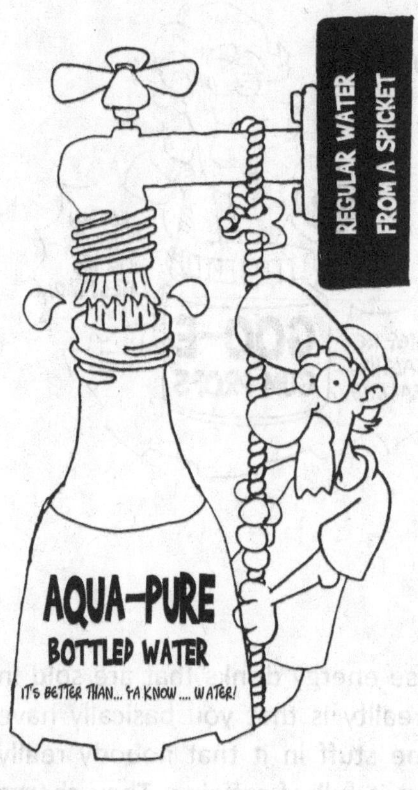

Religion is the same way. Many religions take God's Word and His free gift of salvation and turn into a money making enterprise. They will share sermons that are attractive for you to hear. Instead of telling you about how your sins separate you from God, they will tell you how God is OK with what you are doing. Churches that teach this are more appealing than those churches that preach the truth from God's Word. Are you financially broke? No problem. The church down the road will tell you how God will pour money into your pockets and bless you without you having to change your sinful lifestyle. Also they teach on how you can just name it and claim it. Their theology is making God sound like some kind of genie in a bottle and how He is ready to grant your every wish. Sounds too good to be true, doesn't it? It's because it's deceitful and their congregations are filling up.

The truth is Jesus, the Son of God, was on Earth with a servant attitude. We, as Christians, should model our lives according to how He lived. If He was willing to live a life like that, what makes us any different? Yes, God can and wants to bless us, but first we have to recognize who He is and where we stand before Him. We have to be careful of the deceitful lies that people are sharing with us. Read God's Word for ourselves so that we will know the difference.

Malice (a desire to see others suffer)
According to the Bible, we should love one another. This includes our enemies, too. Finding joy in seeing someone suffer is not cool and goes against what living for Jesus is all about.

But, there are people out there that don't know Jesus and hasn't received His memo note on how to act with one another. People have hate wrapped so tight around their hearts and would love to put some 'butt whoop' on the people that do them wrong. And when they learn that these people are going through some rough times in their life, they sit back and laugh.

God's Word teaches us to love one another, and when we have something against somebody, we should tell them about it and make things right. The next thing you know, people are forgiving each other and everyone lives happily ever after. The end. That sounds like a good and simple plan to me. How about you?

As Christians, we should try our best to live this way. We have to let go of the hate and replace it with love. Instead of enjoying the heartaches of others, you could see if there is something you could do to help. Remember, the best way to get rid of enemies is to turn them into friends.

Gossips
Churches get a bad wrap for being filled with hypocrites and gossipers. And that may have some truth in it. If you think about it, the best way for Satan to tear down a church is to attend it himself. Right?

God tells us to encourage one another and to build each other up. Gossip tears people down with the 'he said, she said' junk. It's not healthy for the body of Christ. We should be about strengthening it up. We should arm ourselves with the ability to recognize when people are gossiping about someone. Here's a simple clue. Their sentences start with "He/she said." or "Let me tell you about what so-and-so did." We should stop gossip at the source and not listen to it. If we don't and we share their bits of information with someone else, we will be considered just as guilty as they are.

Gossip doesn't just happen at church. It happens outside its four walls, too. As Christians, we got to nip it in the bud. Stop doing it. An old saying still applies today, "If you don't have something good to say about somebody, don't say nothing at all." I like that.

Slanderers
This is almost like gossiping, except the person doing it has the intentions of tearing someone down and usually the information about them isn't true. They make up stuff that will harm the person and mess with their credentials as a person. It gives them the appearance of a bad person, regardless of all the good they have done. It's made up of lies and people shouldn't do it.

When people have something to say that's bad about someone, we shouldn't just assume that what they are saying is true. We should find out about them ourselves. We need to know from first hand, not from what someone else has said. What if all court cases were judged based on hear-say only? What if the Defendant never got to plead their case? I believe there would be a lot of innocent people in jail today. Don't you?

If you watch the news, sometimes you will catch a story where a person gets accused of doing something terrible. It could be a teacher that's accused of molesting one of their students. We assume that because the news covers a story on it that it's fact. But, do we really know for sure? Do we really know the person accused? If we heard the news story and then met this person out in public somewhere, we would quickly point them out as a bad person. Wouldn't we? We don't know the true story. We only know what we've been told and we can't base our decision about them until we have heard from them personally. You know? What if the story was made up and this guy was truly innocent? How would you feel then?

God-haters
I can't imagine anyone hating God. That just sounds weird to me. I understand that there are people that don't show reverence to Him or that they choose not to follow Him. But, the fact is there are people out there that flat out hate Him. It's sad considering all that God does in the lives of people that don't think about giving Him credit. So, what or who is a God hater?

To me, it's people that choose to maliciously take God out of things. It's also people that purposely make a joke out of Christianity and everything it stands for. It's when God is mocked and made fun of. That's just wrong.

You've heard of how our country is trying to keep God out of our schools and other government buildings. This is a form of God-hating. Now because of certain laws, preachers and ministers have to be careful about how they address certain sins mentioned in God's Word. Saying the wrong thing about someone could win them a free ticket to jail. Realistically, what is happening is a form of God-hating by hating what His Word says.

Ever watch television that's not on one of them Christian channels? There's a good bit of Jesus-bashing going on through the airwaves or digitally depending on if you are one of the few that still has a TV antenna attached to your house.

It seems like certain shows make it a point to poke fun at Christian stuff for a quick laugh. I'm not talking about your simple funny fat Baptist preacher jokes either. Those are funny. It's where Jesus is portrayed as some kind of freak and he's presented doing things that we know He wouldn't be doing. Why would a show purposely make fun of something like that? I mean I might chuckle if they took a jab at Christian people, but to do it at Jesus? That's God-hating right there! And there's a lot of that on TV and people are getting soaked in by it. If someone were to share the Gospel with them and tell them about Jesus, their first response is going to be to laugh. That's not good!

Keep your eyes open and turn that junk off if it's on your TV at home. At least if Christian folk aren't watching it, they'll lose some ratings and it might get taken off the air.

Insolent (Rude)/Arrogant/Boastful
I know people like this and I just ignore them because I know they don't know any better. But, you really have to wonder what makes them that way. You know?

People are generally rude because they don't care for the feelings of others. That's obvious. But why? It could have been caused from being treated bad by someone themselves and it created a chain reaction. If you think about it, suppose you were mistreated by different people over the years. You would think that most people are like this and you would begin having this 'don't care' attitude when it comes to confrontations and personal relationships with the general public. So what you will be doing is continuing the cycle of a bad behavior. Somebody has to stop the wheel from turning. It may need to happen through you. Being good to others creates positive results.

People with their nose stuck up so high in the air is what I think of when I hear the words arrogance and being boastful. They think they are better than everyone else and tend to look down on others. These people need a pop-knot placed on the side of their head.

The root of this problem could have begun with money and having an abundance of it. Having wealth buys fancy cars, big houses, super cool clothing, and a better education. Sometimes when a person steps out with their blingy-bling and looks upon all that they have, it can go straight to their head. It will then begin to swell. When they meet someone that is less fortunate than they are, they act like roosters and strut their feathers around. I hate to bust their bubble, but they are still no better than we are. We all walk on the same ground, breathe the same air, and in God's eyes we are all the same. As Christians, we can't let money and material things have that kind of foothold in our lives. It was God that gave it to us and He can also take it away. He expects us to be good stewards with it.

Remember, we are saved because God had mercy on us. We were sinners that needed His salvation. We also have a family out there that consists of Christian brothers and sisters. We're family. There are also people out there that need Jesus in their life and they need to hear about Him from you. It's hard for them to listen when your head is in the clouds. Keep that in mind.

Disobeying parents

I have kids and sometimes they try to get out of hand. As a parent, I have to guide and direct them in the correct path. When I give them a job to do, they better do it. And when they don't, it's called being disobedient and it comes with a terrible price. It's called a whoopin'.

The problem we have in the world today is that disciplining your child now has guidelines. They want us to try new disciplinary actions that don't involve physical contact. Spanking your child is now frowned upon, and doing so could result in having your child removed from your home. Kids don't even get paddled in school anymore. What's up with that? I guess a lot has changed over the years. No wonder kids don't listen to their parents or respect authorities anymore. They need their butts tore up!

What does the Bible say about discipline? Ever heard of 'spare the rod, spoil the child'? It's OK to spank your child according to God's Word. They need it when they do wrong. Keeping in mind, we should do it out of love and not from anger. Our reason behind our whoopin' makes all the difference in the world. The positive result will be a kid that will grow up to have respect for others and for their parents.

The Bible tells us that even though these people from the Book of Romans knew how God felt about it, they continued doing it anyway without a care. They knew better! Even today, people know right from wrong. However, some try and justify their wrongness and approve of others that are doing it, too. Let me tell you something. God doesn't like it today the same way He didn't like it back then. He never changed. The sad thing is that God's judgment will be death. Wow! That's some scary stuff! Ain't it?

God's Righteous Judgment
Romans 2: 1-16

A lot of folks are quick to point out the wrong in others. Many times they don't search the person's heart to find out why they are the way they are. And most of the time it's over nick-picking stuff that has nothing to do with that person's salvation or their walk with Christ.

I remember visiting with a local church with my family. I felt a need to help the church grow by stepping in to create ways to bring in more people. The church was in a location that could easily be a light in their community and reach people that wouldn't normally attend church. It would have been great if they were open to new ideas and modern ways of sharing the

Gospel. But they weren't. They were traditional and had a set of rules for doing things. I guess that would explain why they only had a few members.

My kids aren't like your ordinary church kids. They are a little rough around the edges and from looking at them from the outside; I could see why someone would think they needed some Jesus. But, my kids are saved. They have asked for forgiveness of their sins and Jesus lives in their heart. I know this because I was with them when it happened. But from the outside, they look a little worldly. Instead of preppy dress shirts, they wear rock concert shirts. Rather than wearing dress slacks and dress shoes, my kids wear blue jeans and Converse hi-tops. My son wears ear rings. It's no big deal to me because I know where their heart is. But, some of the members were quick to explain to my son how wrong it was for him to wear his desired church attire and how he should change. He was judged.

Because of this finger pointing, he didn't want to go back to this church again. What if my son was lost and didn't know Jesus? These members would have pushed him out the door and back into the world. He would have remained a lost sinner. Needless to say, we never went back to this church.

Judging in this case had a negative result because the person doing it didn't have their act together. God's judgment is based on truth and that truth comes from His Word. Jesus wasn't so concerned with how someone was dressed on the outside. He was all about what was on the inside of a person. I feel it's more important to know if Jesus is in their heart than what a person is wearing. Let God convict people's hearts. Not us.

Now I know there are Christian people out there that are stubbornly being disobedient to God. They choose to go a path that is different than what God has planned. For that, they will be judged. While they live their life the way they want, that goes against God's ways, they will be miserable and will be confronted with troubles. God could go ahead and judge them, but He doesn't. That's because of His patient and kind nature. His hopes are that they will see the errors of their ways and turn back to Him. God is merciful like that.

Have you ever told your kid not to play with electric outlets? I know I have. It's because we know they will get shocked. Right? My kid was stubborn as a child and stuck a set of keys in the outlet in our hallway. Well, the inevitable happened and he got shocked. It scared the stew out of him and he cried out to me. I picked him up and comforted him and reminded him again of why he shouldn't do that. Lesson learned and he has never pulled a stunt like that again. I believe that is how God works. He will let us learn some lessons from our disobedience.

Just be assured that He will be there when you cry out for Him. When you have reached the bottom because of your bad choices in life, you can call out to Him. He will welcome you with open arms. Guaranteed.

The Jews And The Law
Romans 2: 17-29

These guys knew the law. They were also teaching others the law. They understood the rules and regulations, but weren't really living by them. The problem was that they lost their effectiveness as true witnesses for the Lord. People could see right through their hypocritical behavior. They were basically blaspheming God because of the way they represented Him in the world.

This applies to us today. If you're saved, you have a new life. Right? If you are professing to be a Christian, you are telling people that you follow Jesus. Agree? Your life should reflect it.

You know why the people that work at McDoogle wear uniforms? It's because they are to represent the fine burger establishment. If you see them with their uniforms on, you know that they are currently on the clock and are there to serve you. Right?

The Police Department employees serve the public. How do you know when police officers are on duty? It's when they have their uniforms on. If they were in civilian clothes, they would look like the rest of the people in the world. If they tried to arrest you without their uniform on, you wouldn't take them seriously and would ask for proof. You see?

As Christians, we can't just live how we want to. Well, we could, but it wouldn't work out too well. People need to see some proof. How do we show others the proof of who we say we are? Are we living it? Do we speak it? Does our life reflect Jesus?

We are here to represent God to those that don't know Him. This is why it's so important to live according to His Word. Being a Christian isn't just all about us, it's also about us showing Christ to the world.

God's Faithfulness
Romans 3: 1-8

Sin is a serious thing even though many of us take it for granted. I guess we don't realize that it separates us from God. Everyone in the world is guilty and is condemned because of it; you, me, them. We're sinners!

From these verses, you can read where Paul strips down the excuses people have as to why they don't consider themselves a sinner. We can apply this to our lives today. Here are some of our common excuses:

1. I don't believe in God.
2. My conscience is my guide.
3. I'm not so bad. There are others that are worse than me.
4. I go to church and I'm a proud member in good standing.
5. I'm religious.

It's not who we are in society that determines if we are sinners or not. It's our actions, our thoughts, and our nature that goes against God's laws, the Ten Commandments, and following Jesus' standards of perfection. And to be honest, it's impossible for us to be perfect like Jesus. That's why we are saved by faith in Him and not by our works.

As Christians who are saved, we should try our best to live by the example that Jesus set for us when He was here. We can study His life by reading the Bible. It is important that we follow it. The problem many of us have is that we think we can live how we want to because we have the 'salvation ticket'. But, what does God think about this lifestyle? To know this, we would have to know Him.

How do we view God? Unless we know how He feels about sin and that He will judge us for it, we are more likely to take Him for granted, too. Here are some common views we have about God and sin:

1. It's God's job to forgive.
2. God loves us too much that He won't judge us.
3. Sin ain't all that bad. Actually, we can learn some cool lessons from it.
4. I'm just following the latest trends. It's OK to do what I'm doing 'cause everybody's doing it, too.

The fact is God hates sin and wants to remove it. And He is! There is coming a time when He will totally wipe it out from the face of the Earth and we will have to answer to Him for our participation in it. All that junk we do that goes against His standards is the reason we are called sinners. If we haven't asked for forgiveness of our sins and asked Jesus to come live in our hearts, we're doomed.

No One Is Righteous
Romans 3: 9-20

How does that make you feel? Knowing that regardless of all the good things you have done for others or how nice of a person you've been all your life, God considers you a sinner? In His eyes, you are guilty. His judgment on you will be the same as if you committed the worse thing a person could possibly ever do. That stinks! Doesn't it?

You're guilty of sin and so am I. Sin? What are we doing that is so wrong? I'm a good person! I go to church, I read my Bible, and I help the homeless by giving them warm blankets every year in the ministry I'm involved in. I even put money in the offering plate. Big deal!

Look! I don't make the rules. God does! It's because our life doesn't meet up to His standards. Remember the Ten Commandments from Exodus 20: 1-17? Those are God's laws that we should follow and our natural instinct is to break them. The way Jesus lived His life is the standard we should follow. Are we walking the same path? I'm sure that

JUST BECAUSE THEY'RE GOOD, IT DOESN'T MAKE THEM SIN-FREE.

we're not.

It's all of this stuff and our inability to follow it that makes us sinners. You see? But, before we get our bloomers in a wad, let me tell you that there is hope for us. His name is Jesus! His death on the cross and resurrection paved a way for us by building a bridge that allows sinners like us to make things right with Almighty God. Jesus died for our sins folks! That's hope!

Righteousness Through Faith
Romans 3: 21-31

This is the Good News!! From the previous chapters, we realized where we stood before Almighty God. We are sinners doomed and found guilty. No doubt! You with me?

"For all have sinned, and come short of the glory of God..." - *Romans 3: 23*

Did you catch that? What can we do about it? Now we are fixing to learn how we go about getting a pardon for our crimes. Check this out:

Being justified freely by his grace through the redemption that is in Christ Jesus: Whom God hath set forth to be a propitiation through faith in his blood, to declare his righteousness for the remission of sins that are past, through the forbearance of God; To declare, I say, at this time his righteousness: that he might be just, and the justifier of him which believeth in Jesus. - Romans 3: 24-26

What does all that mean? Simply the ones that believe and have faith in Jesus Christ are justified. Basically what happened is God's love came through and now we have a way out. Read this:

For God so loved the world, that he gave his only begotten Son, that whosoever believeth in him should not perish, but have everlasting life. For God sent not his Son into the world to condemn the world; but that the world through him might be saved. - John 3: 16, 17

You see, God saw that no matter how hard we tried to be good, we just can't meet His standards. So, out of His love for humanity, He provided the ultimate sacrifice for sin; His Son Jesus Christ. To save ourselves from sin's destruction, all we have to do is believe in Him. And believing is more than just knowing that He exists.

It's realizing that you're a sinner needing forgiveness and that you're doomed without God's mercy on you. You realize that Jesus is the answer and that you are willing to let Him have control of your life.

You pray to Him, sincerely asking for forgiveness of your sins, and then you simply receive Him. That's faith!

You are now born again. From this point forward, you will begin growing by learning more from His Word and applying it to your life with a goal of becoming like Him. True living has just begun.

Abraham Justified Through Faith
Romans 4: 1-25

Have you ever heard of Abraham? I'm not talking about the tall fella with the funny looking beard that became a President of the United States a long time ago. I mean he's a cool fella and all, but there's a dude from the Bible with the same name.

In the Old Testament, it talks about a guy named Abraham. God had made a promise that He would make nations out of him and that he would have kids. I mean that sounds good and all, but the problem was that Abraham was too old to have kids and his wife was, too. This could have created a problem, but Abraham held onto God's promise. Even though he was an old prune, he had the faith that God would come through with it no matter how the circumstances looked and showed it by his actions. And guess what? God came through just like He said He would. Abraham had kids and nations were built. Abraham believed and trusted in God. And because he did this, God accredited him as being righteous. The Bible tells us that without faith, we cannot please God. Hmm...

So, what's this all about? We went from being called sinners to being saved and now faith? What's that got to do with anything??!!

As a Christian, life here on out will be lived on faith. Faith is simply trusting and believing in God. Our goal is to become righteous and this can only be justified by having faith in Him.

The day you got saved, you showed faith by trusting and believing in Jesus Christ and what He did on the cross for you. You made that step forward in faith by asking Him to come into your life and forgive you. You sincerely felt sorry for all of the junk you've done, and out of faith, you turned to Jesus. That is faith right there!

God's promise to you about your salvation is found in the verse ahead:

For whosoever shall call upon the name of the Lord shall be saved. - Romans 10: 13

Just as in Abraham's situation, God keeps His promises. And

that's a guarantee!

Peace And Joy
Romans 5: 1-11

By His grace we are justified before Him. Because of Jesus Christ and our faith in Him, God has forgiven us of all the junk we have done. There is peace in knowing that. We should be happy!

Think about it! You no longer have to worry about facing God's judgment on you for all the wrong you did. You will be found innocent. All that stuff that separated you from God has been washed away. When you hear people talking about being washed in the blood of Jesus, they are not being gross. What this means is simply that we are made clean by what Jesus suffered on the cross when He shed His blood for us. That's where the blood comes from. That should get you excited! The rest of our life should be pumped up as we await His return because

now we're ready!

As Christians, however, we shouldn't just be sitting around waiting on Jesus to come back. We are encouraged from God's Word to be actively moving by learning more about Him, sharing what we learn with others, and growing spiritually to become like

Him. We do this by reading the Bible, going to church, talking about Him with people and sharing the light of Jesus in our lives through the way we act in the world. It all doesn't just happen over night. It's all a growing process. And God helps us with it through life's experiences.

Being a Christian doesn't mean we are going to have a trouble-free life. Oh no! We're going to go through some junk. Many times it will feel like God drops a fifty pound brick on top of our shoulders from Heaven. We will suffer through some things, but God always helps us through it. These are called trials and valleys. Ever heard of that before? They're awful!

Personally, I don't like having to go through them, but I know that God uses these bad things in my life to build my character and to make me stronger in my faith in Him. He allows us to suffer because we learn to depend on Him more than we do on ourselves. Over time we will develop this 'God's got it!!' attitude whenever a problem comes because we will know without a doubt that He does. And He will always provide us a way out. That's some cool stuff! That's what I love about being saved. Because of what Jesus did for me on the cross, I am reconnected to God. Even when I was living life at my worst, He loved me and died for me. He died for you, too. It doesn't matter what bad you have done, He loves you and wants to be your Provider and Problem Solver to all of your life's junk. We can turn

41

to Him for everything. That should make you happy right there!

Death Through Adam, Life Through Christ
Romans 5: 12-21

When you read the Book of
Genesis, you'll learn that the
first man ever created by
God was this dude named
Adam. He may have been
your average-lookin' fella;
average height, weight, and
healthy. I mean, if you think
about it, none of the food
that God provided him had
the junk in it that food has
today. It was straight out of
the garden. He may have
even had 'no tan lines'

DEATH THROUGH ADAM - LIFE THROUGH CHRIST

because Adam had to walk around all day without any clothes
on. The dude had it made in the shade and probably lived the
simple life.

God didn't want Adam to be all by himself. Yes, he had animals
walking around freely to look at. But, this would be sorta like
hanging out at the zoo everyday and I'm sure this got kinda
boring day in and day out. He needed some companionship. Who
wants to hang out with a bunch of animals all the time anyway?
So God made him a woman and used Adam's rib to do it.
This woman's name was Eve. Knowing that God's ways are
perfect in all that He does for us, I could only imagine that she
was beautiful and probably all that Adam had ever hoped for. I
would almost guarantee that she didn't complain or nag, had

dinner ready every day, kept the home cleaned, and might have even massaged his toes after he had been walking around all day petting animals. I added that to be funny. I'm sure she was perfect and life was just peachy.

God had given Adam the freedom to take freely of everything that God had provided him with one exception. He warned Adam not to take from this certain little tree He had planted in a remote area of the garden. That shouldn't be a problem, especially when you have all that you need right there in front of you. Right? Wrong! In walks Satan!

Satan tempts the happy couple into disobeying God's command. They 'bite' into it and everything has went down hill ever since. Adam and Eve became separated from God. This is where sin originated and all the junk you see going on in the world today roots back to that day in the garden. Adam and Eve messed up! And the world has been paying the price ever since. That stinks!

People have been trying to reconnect to God through making attempts to follow His laws and making sacrifices for their sins against Him. I picture this process as a ladder that stretches upward to God. People may have gone up a couple of steps, but when they sin, they fall back down to the ground again. It's hard to make it to the top.

God's way through His Son, Jesus, makes it simple and easy. By accepting Him as our Lord and Savior, He lifts us up into God's presence. This is like an elevator ride to God. No more ladders and steps! It's pretty simple!

Because of what Jesus did for us on the cross, He offers us life. Abundant life! All we have to do is take it. You want it? Ask Him for it! It's that simple.

Dead To Sin, Alive In Christ
Romans 6: 1-14

When you think of sin and being a slave to it reminds me of someone being in prison. Don't you? Now, I have never been in prison, but I imagine it ain't the best place in the world to be. I'm sure it's not a vacation resort or even like a few rounds of putt putt golf at one of them fun and fancy places. I just know that I don't want to be there.

The things I have learned about prison is from what I have seen on TV. My wife likes watching them cops' shows and I'm forced to watch them with her because I can't figure out how to work the remote. So, from what I've seen, it's like you're chained down. You can't go anywhere except within those cells. You got people telling you what you can and can't do. Plus, you're forced to wear the same style clothes every day. And orange ain't my color! The

44

only fun you might get comes from watching TV and lifting weights all day. To me, that ain't fun!

I'm trying to think of a time when I felt chained down to something. The only time that comes to my mind is when I worked in an office cubicle for 14 years. You thought I was going to say when I got married, didn't you? Nope! My wife reads my books and I ain't going there! Anyway, back to the cubicle. Every day I reported for work, clocked in, and sat at a desk for eight hours. This was my daily routine. It was me, a phone and a computer. That's it! I didn't even get a window to look outside and see the real world. I was confined to these manufactured walls around me. Pretty sad, huh?

Sin is ugly like that! You become trapped. It begins on the inside of you and works its way outward. It tangles you up like a vine and literally owns you and directs you. It tells you what to do and you become a slave to it.

Being born again releases you from those chains of sin. You begin focusing more on Jesus and living for Him. You become free! Your old ways of thinking begin changing. It's like a light bulb goes off inside you and exposes all the garbage in your life and you start taking the steps to remove it. You see your sins for what they are and you no longer want to be part of it. This change that is taking place is called sanctification. It's like taking a spiritual bath with soap and water. And it even cleans the back of your ears.

These verses talks of being baptized. You know what that's all about, right? It's an outward expression of your new birth in Jesus. In some churches, you and a preacher get to stand in an over-sized tub of water. He tells you to hold your nose while he dunks you in and you go under. People are watching this. You stay under for a few seconds, depending on if the preacher likes you, and then he brings you

back up. Now the people are cheering you on! You just shared with them this 'new you'. Pretty cool, huh?

You are no longer a slave to sin, but that doesn't mean that Satan won't try to tempt you back into it again. Your old ways will try and resurface, but you have Jesus now. He will help you along the way and you should try your best to stay as close to Him as possible. You become weak to temptation when you step off of the path that Jesus puts you on. The key here is to stay on it. Keep your eyes on Him.

Slaves To Righteousness
Romans 6: 15-23

The key verse from this scripture is the last one: *"For the wages of sin is death; but the gift of God is eternal life through Jesus Christ our Lord."*

Stay away from sin. It's like a poison and comes with a terrible price. It's death! God has a better idea; a gift of eternal life to those that want it. It's through Jesus Christ and following His path of righteousness. To put that in simple terms, surrender your life to Him and turn from all that junk you used to do and start living better according to what He tells us in the Bible.

That's pretty much it in a nut shell.

When a person gets saved, they are promised eternal life after this current one is over and done with. But, while we are here, we can live and should live according to God's Word. It just makes living more fun and more worthwhile. We should start looking for ways to represent Jesus in the world by helping people and loving them. We could begin using our gifts and talents that God gave us for His glory. Take a look at yourself. What could you be doing for the Lord today, tomorrow, and the rest of your life? Then, just do it.

An Illustration From Marriage
Romans 7: 1-6

These verses talk about the laws that the Jews were following pretty closely. These laws were given to Moses by God. Yes, they offered everyone a better way of living, but people had a hard time following them. The struggle was with their old nature. Many felt that as long as they tried to follow these laws, it brought them closer to God. But it didn't. Actually, it made many realize their sins and their helpless feeling of not being able to do anything about it.

Paul uses the illustration of marriage to show how they were bound to their laws. Just like in marriage, the only way to be able to marry someone else was for their former spouse to die. The same is true for them, they basically had to die spiritually to be released from the law and be born again spiritually through faith in Jesus Christ. This is how they are to be made right in the sight of God. This applies to us, too.

When Jesus died on the cross and rose again, it symbolizes how our old nature dies and we are born again when we ask Him to come into our life and save us. We begin living on faith in Him instead of being bound to our sin.

I know all that sounds technical and strange, but the lesson here is that because of faith in Jesus, we're not bound to anything. We are free. Sin and death has no hold on us. We are guaranteed eternal life. We don't earn it or work in order to get it by following a list of rules and good deeds. Like I said, it's free! We're set free!

The sad thing in the world today is that there are a lot of people trying to earn their Salvation. Yes, they are probably the nicest people you would ever want to meet, but are they saved? Ask them. Ask yourself. The way to know for sure is if you or they have prayed and sincerely asked for forgiveness of their sins and asked Jesus to save them.

It's that simple. Going to church and following the Golden Rules won't get them there. It'll just make them better people. It's best to know for sure.

Struggling With Sin
Romans 7: 7-25

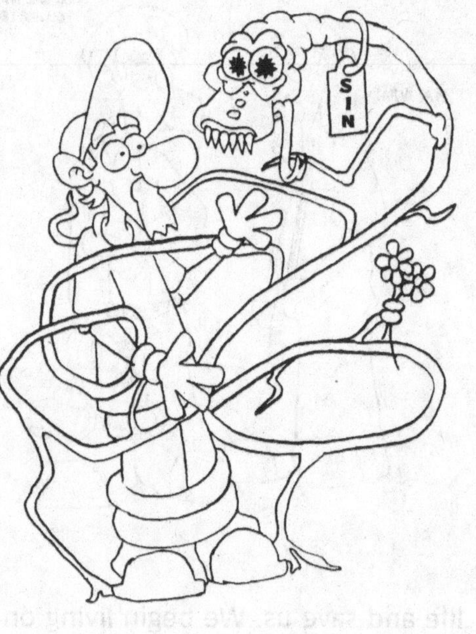

Paul realized the struggles that went on in people's lives. The desire to sin is like right there! How do we know what sin is? It's anything that goes against God that is written in His Word. When we realize that He is against that thing we do, we realize that it is a sin. We also realize that it is a struggle to keep from doing it.

People may try their best to not do it in order to make things right with God, but it's not going to work. That's why Paul was excited by what Jesus did for him on the cross. He knew his nature was to sin, but because of his faith in Jesus, he knew that he was forgiven.

Did you know that we are naturally born to sin? It is naturally our instinct to go against God by the way we live our life. That's bad! This applies to both the saved and unsaved person. Just because a person is saved doesn't mean they won't sin in some kind of way. It's human nature. If a person were to simply compare their lives to the Ten Commandments, they will see how 'not perfect' they really are. That's why it's important to know whether Jesus is living on the inside or not. Because of Him, we are forgiven.

Life Through The Spirit
Romans 8: 1-17

As Christians, we battle with our sinful nature to live our life in the Spirit. Now that isn't some kind of weird religious experience I'm talking about. Living in the Spirit to me basically means living your life 'souled out' to God. To do so would mean to focus on Him during everyday situations, to add more of Him in our day-to-day activities, and serve Him according to how He says to do it in His Word. That's not too weird, is it?

When we do this, a lot of our sinful ways will begin to fade away. We won't be controlled by it because we won't be thinking about it. Our minds will be on God and on what He wants us to be doing. You see what I'm saying?

The problem many Christians have in life is that they catch themselves doing some of the old things they used to do. Why is it? Because they allowed it back into their life and focused on it again. They may have pushed God to the side for a minute and forgot to bring Him back in. When we do this, it opens the door for temptations to overpower us because we stepped out of God's will.

Cats are good at killing mice, right? I imagine a person that has a cat for a pet around the house rarely has problems with mice. Why? Well, because the cat is there. Mice hate cats. The same is true with sin. As long as we allow more of God in our life, the less of a threat temptation will have against us. Did you catch that?

WHEN YOU PUT MORE 'JESUS' IN THE MIX,
THERE'S LESS ROOM FOR TEMPTATION.

To help ourselves with the battle of our sinful nature would be to focus more on 'Jesus stuff'. Make every effort to put more of your attention on Him than all that junk that's in the world. Try it!

Another thing I got from these verses is that, as Christians, we are children of God. Do you realize how cool that is? We're not a bunch brainless 'sheeple' following a crap-load of religious stuff! We are God's kids and that comes with some cool fringe benefits. We are heirs to the King! Can you take that all in mentally? Can you dig it?

Because of that very fact means we are not bound to the worries of this world. We can live in victory knowing that our Father in Heaven is looking out for us. He's got our backs! That's enough to get you all excited right there!

Future Glory
Romans 8: 18-27

The world is going downhill so fast and falling apart at the seams. This place is a mess! It's worse than my teenager's bedroom. Awful! What you see in the world today is a product of sin and it's only going to get worse. It's sorta like that potato that fell and hid itself in the pantry. It will slowly rot.

Eventually it will turn into mush and stink up the whole house for weeks. And there won't be enough 'smell good spray' to get rid of the stink.

Even in our bodies, we are slowly dying, too. I know that is a sad thing to think about but it's true. Look around you and see everybody that has some kind of illness going on in their body. Look at the tombstones and see all the people that have passed on in death. It is a sad thing to think about but it's the reality of life.

If you're living for the Lord like I am, you have hope. Jesus is coming back for us one day. We don't know when, regardless of what people that predict it may say. But, we have the hope that He is. The Holy Spirit confirms it in our souls as we patiently wait.

As we wait, we will carry on with living and going through all of the junk that living has to offer. But, you know, the Holy Spirit is our Comforter. He is there to keep us going. He lives within us to pick us up when we're down. Even when we are too tired and weary from the fight, He will pray for us and give us the right words to say. He is on our side to help us through it all.

I look at life as if it were a boxing match. First few rounds, we may throw some good punches and sit down when the bell rings. Our coach, the Holy Spirit, gives us a spiritually refreshing water drink, pep talk, and some strategic fighting tips. The next thing you know we're back in the ring fighting again. Yes, we will get some bruises and cuts, but the key is to keep on fighting. It's not over until Jesus returns.

More Than Conquerors
Romans 8: 28-39

The bottom line is this: God loves us! He sent His Son to die on the cross for us. He will save you!

To be honest, it doesn't matter what you think of yourself. You may lack self confidence. You may think you are not good enough. It doesn't matter! God loves you! You may have lived your life with people treating you like a piece of crap, calling you names, and making you feel like yesterday's trash. God cares! He cares for you!

Knowing that the Creator of Heaven and Earth, that made everything in it, loves you should make you feel all tingly inside. And you should. That means He is approachable by you. If you're not saved today, you can pray in confidence knowing that He is listening and wants to save you. He doesn't care about your past or the things you have done. He only cares about you.

I love the verses 38 and 39 :

"For I am persuaded, that neither death, nor life, nor angels, nor principalities, nor powers, nor things present, nor things to come, Nor height, nor depth, nor any other creature, shall be able to separate us from the love of God, which is in Christ Jesus our Lord."

If that ain't conformation of His love for you, I don't know what is.

God's Sovereign Choice
Romans 9: 1-29

I have always heard that the Jewish people from Israel were God's chosen ones. I

had always thought that they belonged to God and would one day live happily ever after with Him simply because God put His Heavenly branding iron on them, but today I learned that this isn't necessarily true.

Paul is still writing his letter to the Romans, and in these verses, he talks about the people of Israel. Yes, God made a covenant with Abraham and his descendants. But according to Paul's letter (verses 6 and 7), just because a person descended from Israel doesn't mean they are a part of Israel or a descendant of Abraham. Wow! That could get confusing! If you think about it, a person could simply do an ancestry search on the internet or 'scroll search' back in those days, and if Abraham's name was on their family tree branch, they were good. If not, they were in trouble. I imagine a lot of Jews felt they had special privileges because they were part of Abraham's family tree, but here we learn that they didn't.

It's all about God's mercy. We learn a little something about God beginning in verse 14 and it talks about His mercy. To be right before God, it doesn't depend on our desires and efforts, but on His mercy. God has mercy on which He chooses and hardens the ones He wants to harden. His mercy isn't something we work towards or manipulate in our own efforts. It's all Him!

You see, God has this planned out ahead of time. He knows who will be saved and who won't. It's not that he only selects certain people. Instead, he knows years ahead in advance into the future and knows who will reach out to Him. The ones that will never want to be saved, He may use them for His purpose in reaching the ones that will. Does that make sense? It's sorta like the story of Moses and Pharaoh. Pharaoh had the hardened heart, right? God used him to reach the others.

A lesson from all of this could be the fact that 'being saved' isn't a genetic thing. Just because your Grandpa Scooter is a Christian, it doesn't make you one. The only blood that's gonna work for you is the blood of Jesus. And again, a person isn't saved by works, but by God's mercy. It just doesn't work that way. But, by His mercy, salvation is available to anyone that wants it.

Israel's Unbelief
Romans 9: 30- 10: 21

I get the understanding that the people of Israel just didn't get it. These folks were religious people - no doubt. They did all the cool stuff that religious people do. They went to church, read their laws, and did their best to follow them the best they could. They even popped others on the back of the neck for not doing it. But, they missed the mark. Where was God in all of this? I mean they were busy following His rule book, but never saw the love He shared through it. They didn't get the love letter relationship that God wanted them to read.

The thing that keeps coming out from the past few chapters is how works don't save you. It's faith in Jesus Christ. Even when Jesus, God in the flesh, was walking with them, they didn't recognize Him. And yet, they knew their religion pretty good and even persecuted Jesus and accused Him of not following it, too.

Dude, they were confused!

To me this is similar to churches out there practicing their religion and thinking they got it goin' on. And believe me, there are several religions out there and they continue to branch out to even more. But, here's the deal! It's not going to save you!

Just like in the old days when people wore sandals and drove camels, God still wants that relationship with us. One day we got to put that religion stuff down and ask ourselves, "Do I know God on a personal level? Have I confessed Him as Lord of my life?"

The key verses here are:

That if thou shalt confess with thy mouth the Lord Jesus, and shalt believe in thine heart that God hath raised him from the dead, thou shalt be saved. For with the heart man believeth unto righteousness; and with the mouth confession is made unto salvation. - Romans 10: 9, 10

This is where it's at! It's when you reach a point where you realize where you stand before God – a sinner doomed to His wrath because of your sin. To make things right before Him, you don't go and try and do some good deeds. You don't just start going to church every week. You take your sins and your guilt of being a sinner to Jesus in prayer and you ask for forgiveness of them. Out of trust and faith in Him, you believe in what He has done for you on the cross and in His resurrection. And then you accept Him into your heart and confess Him as Lord of your life. That's salvation!

You will continue living your life growing closer to Him by learning through life lessons, learning from reading and hearing His Word, praying and living on faith in Him. That's pretty simple. Ain't it? Religion just makes it too hard.

The Remnant Of Israel
Romans 11: 1-10

God chose the Jews to spread His news of salvation to the world. Paul, the writer of this book, was a Jew. The disciples and most of the early missionaries were Jews, too. But, as we already know, being a Jew doesn't guarantee their salvation. It's by faith alone. And the faithful Jews that believed in God's message of salvation were considered 'the remnant'.

Many of the Jews had a hardened heart toward the Gospel. They rejected it and would be punished for it. Even today, there are people that simply don't want to hear any of the 'Jesus' stuff. Maybe you have met someone like that. You can recognize them because they will be the ones running from you when you invite them to church or who begins flinching with what seems like a nervous disorder when you start talking about God around them. These folks have hardened hearts. The only One that can break that hardness is God's Holy Spirit that will deal with them on a personal level. All you have to do is pray for them.

These remnants mentioned in these verses knew that they were saved, not because of their nationality, religion, or family tree. It was by the grace of God. Grace? You hear that a lot in Christianity, but what is that? Even though there are several books out there that speak of grace and even some that have hundreds of pages just on that subject, I can only describe it in a few sentences. Sorry, but I like simple!

Grace to me is like loving your kids even though they are rebellious and don't want to do what you tell them to do. Yet, you still love them anyway. Even though they act like a bunch of monkeys, you allow them to stay in your house and eat up your bananas. And the reason you allow them to live there is because they recognize you as their Dad and that you know they don't know any better. It's by your grace that keeps them from being tossed out on their heads.

Now some of your kids have gone too far and decided they don't want to live with you and have told you many times to leave them alone. They don't want any part of you and have basically disowned you as their Dad. You are forced to let them have their way and move on. The sad thing for them is that you have planned a permanent vacation for your family. And the sad thing is that these kids won't get to go. Hopefully, they will reconcile their differences with you before it's too late.

Was that a pretty good illustration of grace?

Engrafted Branches
Romans 11: 11-24

Paul paints a cool picture of God's family by illustrating words describing an olive tree with its branches. I personally don't know what an olive tree looks like, so I will choose a familiar

vision of a pine tree or maybe an oak. Try and picture it with me!
You got this tree and it has a lot of branches sticking out. You see
it? OK. This would represent God's plan for the Jews. The Jews
are the branches and the root of the tree is Jesus. Are you with
me so far? Unfortunately, some of the Jews chose not to believe
in all of this 'Jesus' stuff. Try picturing branches falling off the
tree. This represents those people.

The Gospel went out to the
Gentiles. These were
people that weren't Jews,
but chose to put their faith
in Jesus. For every new
believing Gentile, stick a
new branch in the tree.
Kinda lick the bottom of it
so that it will stick. These
are considered the
engrafted branches that
the verses are talking
about.

Now let's say that some of
those unbelieving Jews
changed their minds. They
have decided to put their
faith in Jesus. Well, lick the bottom of a few more branches to
engraft them into the tree again. Even though they were part of
the original plan, their faith is what puts them into the tree.
Make sense? That's what Paul was trying to share with
everybody.

Here again, it's a faith thing.

All Israel Will Be Saved
Romans 11: 25-32

Verse 26: *"And so all Israel shall be saved:..."*

There are some speculations as to what this verse means. Is it saying that many of the Jews in the last generation will get their

hearts right and turn to Jesus? Or does Israel have a spiritual meaning that includes everyone that's saved – Gentiles and Jews? Or does it mean that everybody living in the country of Israel have a stamped guarantee that they are cool with God regardless of the stuff they have done against Him when He comes back? Man, that's tricky!

For me, I'm going to take the simple approach and look back to the previous verses that spoke of the tree and its branches. If the branches were those that put their faith in Jesus Christ (Jews and Gentiles) and the root represented Jesus, what about that tall part that sticks up out of the ground that the branches and root are attached to? What would that be? Maybe that represents Israel in the spiritual sense. If that's the case, then many unbelieving Jews are in trouble!

To put that in a broader sense, if you're not saved, you're basically a bunch loose branches lying on the ground. And we know what happens to loose branches when it's time to clean your yard up. That's a scary thought, ain't it?

Doxology
Romans 11: 33-36

These last three verses of this chapter are considered a doxology. Personally, I didn't have a clue what that word meant and didn't know it was even in the dictionary. But, it is! And today we get to learn a new word.

A doxology is a prayer of praise to God for the wisdom of His plan. Paul must have gotten a few Jesus bumps down his spine when he got to this part of his letter and decided to give a 'shout out' to God. And that's cool!

O the depth of the riches both of the wisdom and knowledge of God! how unsearchable are his judgments, and his ways past finding out! For who hath known the mind of the Lord? or who hath been his counsellor? Or who hath first given to him, and it shall be recompensed unto him again? For of him, and through him, and to him, are all things: to whom be glory for ever. Amen.
- Romans 11: 33-36

That just goes to show you that it's OK to praise God whenever you feel the need to. Sometimes you just can't help yourself.

I remember times singing songs in church and having to stop to have a moment with God to tell Him how awesome He is. Yes, I did it in front of people and I felt a little weird at first, but I did it anyway. People were looking at me, but they knew what I was doing. Now that I think back on it, they probably received a better blessing from it than hearing my screeching voice.

Any time is a good time to praise God and tell Him how great He is. It may be meant for that someone who is watching you. Who knows?

Living Sacrifices
Romans 12: 1-8

According to Paul, we have a job to do. We have job security! Paul encourages us to offer our bodies as a living sacrifice that is holy and pleasing to God because this is our spiritual act of worship. Say what? That doesn't sound like a job! Actually, we worship God by becoming walking vessels for His glory. Everything we say and do should point others to Him. If we do this with the right heart, it doesn't become a job. Instead, we are offering ourselves and living for His purposes and not our own. You could call this new lifestyle as being 'souled out' to Jesus. And it doesn't just happen overnight.

This change starts by the renewing of your mind. We are no longer to be focused on worldly junk and the way it does things. We should be paying close attention to God's Word and on the example Jesus left us when He was here. With this new way of thinking, you will begin seeing what God's perfect plan is for your life. You will see what it is that He wants you to do and what your purpose is on this big ol' planet. This is when life starts getting exciting!

You know those talents and skills you have that you may not be using right now? Well, now that you are living 'souled-out' to Jesus, you will be able to use them. That's why God gave them to you. And you thought all this time it was for your benefit. Not hardly! It's for God's glory and He will show you what to do with them.

Now don't get the big-head thinking that you're all special and stuff. I mean, you are special, but so are the thousands of other Christians out there doing the same thing. The key here is knowing that you are a part of a team of believers with the same focus in mind. We're doing the will of God; serving and reaching folks! Don't let pride kick in when you are serving the Lord. It just ain't cool!

Love
Romans 12: 9-21

These verses sum up the basics of Christian living right here. I would like to talk about them briefly for a minute in simple words:

Love must be sincere
Love is more than just saying it. It's usually followed by an action. If you really love someone, you'll stand by them through thick and thin. You'll treat folks a lot nicer and look past their faults.

Hate what is evil/cling to what is good
When you see or hear something that goes against God or how
He wants us to live, you'll walk away from it. You won't take part
in it. You will want to be more involved in things that glorify God
and promotes good values.

Brotherly love
Do you have naturally born brothers and sisters? You love them,
right? Well, pretend like you do. Seriously though, this is the
same type of love that we should have for our Christian brothers
and sisters. You will stand beside them and be there for them in
their times of need.

Honor one another above yourselves
Jesus came as a servant to others. We should have the same
attitude and never think that we are better than someone else.
Put them first. If you want a quick crash course, do like Jesus did
and wash someone's feet. It's Biblical and it works!

Never lack zeal/keep spiritual fervor
We should be enthusiastic or 'on fire' when it comes to serving
God and others. We should never go at it with a dreaded attitude
as if someone made us do it. It defeats the purpose and with that
negative attitude, we may as well stay at home. Get pumped up!

Joyful in hope
To me, this means always keeping a positive attitude and being
happy. Look for the good in everything. Show the world your
teeth every now and then by smiling more. No teeth? No
problem. Show the world your gums!

Patient in affliction
Patience is probably the hardest thing to learn, but we can do it.
When troubles come into our life, just know that God has it

under control. Wait patiently for Him to respond. If you prayed about it, He heard ya.

Faithful in prayer
Pray every day and several times a day if you feel like it. Don't be one of those that only participates in prayer when someone else does all the talking. Get involved! Talk to God! He would like to hear from you.

Share with God's people in need
We are told to help Christian people out. We should because they are our brothers and sisters in the Lord. It could be with money or our time. The next time you hear of someone needing help, see what it is they need help with and be the one to volunteer. Be the one that says, "Pick me! Pick me!"

Practice hospitality
Have you ever been to a get together with family where everyone met at someone's house? Well, the person that owns the house is being hospitable by letting y'all hang out there. We should practice the same mind set when we meet people. Be nice to them with welcome arms.

Bless and do not curse
Instead of fussing people out all the time or causing a stink, try being a blessing to them. Be a positive influence in their life.

Rejoice and mourn
Share the happy times and sad times with others. If they're happy, join in on the laughs. If they're sad, shed a tear with them and give them comfort. And big hugs are good, too!

Living in harmony
It's all about living in peace. Whatever it takes to create peace in

all circumstances, we should make it our goal to do it. If you see folks arguing, don't pick a side. Actually, it would be better if you could work with them together to solve the problem.

Don't be proud
Pride comes before the fall! Try not to think about yourself all the time. It's not all about you. If we go through life thinking about others more often, we shouldn't become a victim of being prideful.

Don't be conceited
Hey look! We're no better than anyone else! We should get our nose out of the air and realize we're on the same planet. We're human! Let's get off of our high horse.

Do not pay evil for evil
Turn the other cheek. If someone does you wrong, don't seek revenge. It will just make matters worse. Just let it go! Respond with being nice. It will throw them for a loop.

Do what is right in people's eyes
People are watching us. Let's give them something good to look at. We should reflect Jesus in our lives by the way we act and talk. Think of your kids that look up to you. You're setting the example in their life.

Live at peace with everyone

This is pretty much the same as living in harmony. Life just flows a lot better when folks ain't arguing or yelling at each other all the time. That would be more like a bad marriage before Jesus steps in.

Do not take revenge (that's God's job)

People are going to try and make us mad. They will do things out of spite and may even try to harm us. We should leave the results in God's hands and leave it alone. He will work it for our good.

Overcome evil by doing good

We are going to get tempted at times to do wrong. It's normal. When we recognize this temptation, we should immediately do something right to counteract the impulse. You know what I mean? Throw evil a curve ball by doing the opposite.

Submission To The Authorities
Romans 13: 1-7

These are some pretty interesting verses written by Paul. They tell us to submit ourselves to our government and the ones in charge over us. This would even include our President. Imagine that!

I remember back when I was a little kid learning what a President was and what his responsibilities were. Before that, I thought they were just old people that were

important enough to have their heads stamped on our money. Now I know that they are actually more than that, even though I may have my opinions about some of them.

It's sorta funny to me that every time we have a Presidential election in the U.S., not only do we get a new President, but we also get another leader to make fun of. I don't think there has ever been one that comedians didn't take a jab at. And when they're done, half the world thinks they are a bunch of funny guys with suits and ties on. Just in my lifetime there was Carter, Reagan, Bush I, Clinton, Bush II, and now Obama. Did we take any of these guys seriously? Really? Definitely not! There's no respect and all the jokes about them make it hard for us to.

These verses tell us that God puts these authorities in place, so regardless of what we think about them, God put them there. They are part of His plan. God expects us to submit to them. Basically, go by the rules that our government comes up with and that they are for our good. I'm cool with that! If you think about it, being a rebellious anti-government flag waving Christian doesn't look too good anyway.

I guess for the Christian, we get a feeling that we only should only follow the lifestyle plans that God has for us. And since we are just visitors here, we may feel a sense of rebellion against this rotten sinful world we live in. But according to God's Word, we should submit

to the authorities because God is using them. We should play by
their rules in their own game. This includes paying taxes, their
salaries, and giving them respect and honor. It's all in God's
design.

Love, For The Day Is Near
Romans 13: 8-14

PAY YOUR DEBTS, BUT NOT THE DEBT OF LOVE!

From this we read that Paul is telling the Romans that the day is drawing near. He is referring to Jesus' return; our day of salvation. Each day is a day closer. He was telling them, until that day comes, to pay their debts, but not their debt of love. Love?

Most of the Ten Commandments, if not all, could be covered by everyone expressing their love; love to God, love to others and love to themselves. Love is one of those emotional and physical things that works pretty good everywhere its applied. If you really loved your neighbor, you wouldn't steal from him, murder him, and cheat with his wife. If you loved God, you would follow His commandments and wouldn't put anything above Him. And if you loved yourself, maybe you would keep a positive attitude and have a better outlook on life. It's cool how love works. We can learn more about how to love by drawing closer to God because, as the scriptures read, God is love.

You could tell Paul had some wisdom going on. I think he also recognized that his world was changing. He saw the sin around him and knew that it would eventually get worse. He gave them a wake-up call and wanted them to focus on the fact that Jesus was returning. He wanted them to be ready. This meant turning from satisfying the desires of their sinful nature. Oh yes, he gave them a list.

The message is true for us today. We gotta quit messing around. If you're saved today, quit dabbling in all that junk the world has to offer. Jesus is returning. We need to be found clean. We need to use our time here to reach out to others that don't know Him.

Try and think of the situation like this. When the day arrives when Jesus comes through the clouds, those that are saved will be caught up in the air to meet Him. As we look down, we'll see the faces of those we had opportunities to witness to, but didn't. How will that make us feel? Did we truly love them? Now it's too late.

The Weak And The Strong
Romans 14: 1-13

From reading these verses, Paul was sharing the fact that Jesus is all about unity. We're Christians because we all follow Christ. We should all be working together for the same common goals, not separated. If you look around you in the world today, you will see the many religions that fall under the Christian category. Each one should have Jesus as the center of its worship. He should be the focal point of all the churches claiming to be Christian. We should all be united based on this fact, but we're not. Each church has its own little extras that make it different than the rest. These extras don't mean a hill of beans to Jesus. Let me tell you that!

Jesus could care less about what denomination you are and what extra stuff you practice or believe as long as you have the most important fact in common. That fact is that Jesus bore the sins of the world and died on the cross for everybody. By doing this, we can be forgiven of our junk when we ask Him to forgive us of it and out of faith ask Him to live in our hearts. If your church or denomination is telling folks that, you're good. Everything else is just extra.

If you like jumping pews every Sunday morning, that's cool. You don't have to and it doesn't add any value to your salvation. If you're services is similar to attending a football game with cheering, clapping, and high-fiving, I think that's awesome. Ya know, whatever rocks your boat! The key here is having that one focal point.

The problem we have in churches and in people is when they think they are ones that have 'being a Christian' all together and all the rest are doing it wrong. They start pointing fingers and begin putting the others down because of the extra stuff that they do. There's no need in all that. We should ask God to give us the spirit of unity, which means having the ability to overlook the extra stuff and realizing we have that one focal point in common.

We, as Christian brothers and sisters in the Lord, not in denomination preference, should work together. If we do something that would offend somebody, let's not do it. We don't want to be a stumbling block for someone. Even if we know it's OK for us to do it, don't do it around them. That's easy enough. Ain't it?

One thing I have learned is that what may be wrong (or a sin) for others may not be wrong to someone else. Each of us should have our own relationship going on with God and we all will give account to Him one day personally. We can't go around preaching our convictions off on someone else. Some things are self-explanatory as to what sin is in the Bible. If the Bible is silent, then it is the Holy Spirit that will convict the hearts of individuals and it shouldn't be us doing it. You hear what I'm saying? There's so much of that going on in the church today and it makes me sick. Leave people alone! Love them like God tells us to and let Him deal with their hearts. When we are pointing fingers, we are basically pointing them in the direction of the exit door. You know?

Paul, The Minister To The Gentiles
Romans 15: 14-22

In these verses, Paul encourages his readers to instruct others. We can take this as a personal message to us to do the same. We should be willing to share all that we have learned from God's Word, our experiences with God, and our faith with people we know and even people we don't know. This could be with our family and friends.

And if you're bold enough, share it with someone you meet for the first time at Wally World. That's what it's all about!

Paul includes again his purpose and mission for doing what he does. His ambition was not for personal gain but was for divine purposes. He was serving God. We should be doing it for the right reasons, too. There are many ministers out there that are sharing the Gospel for money and personal recognition. This is called selfish ambition. This ain't cool!

As we go out into the world proclaiming God's Word to others, our heart needs to be in it for God. Our purpose, just like Paul's, should be for God's glory, not ours. We should treat all that we do for Him as an act of worship and sacrifice. When we do it this way, God will bless it and use you to carry out His work here on Earth. Then, our ambition will become 'holy ambition' and that's the right kind of ambition to have.

Paul's Plan To Visit Rome
Romans 15: 23-33

The only thing that I get from reading this is the fact that Paul wanted to go to Rome, but he had other places to go to first. Can you imagine what that was like? He could have stopped his ministry work for a little bit to go, but he was so

focused on what God had called him to do. He had a passion to see people get saved. He wanted to 'go where no man had gone before' to share the Gospel. We should also share that same passion for Jesus and the lost in this world. Putting aside the things we want to do and serve the Lord wherever He takes us is the life of a person that is 'souled out' to Jesus. Could we be like that?

We learn from Acts 28 that Paul finally gets to go to Rome.

Unfortunately, it wasn't for recreational reasons or while on vacation. He went as a prisoner with roaming benefits. I'm glad to know that God allowed him to finally see it. God knows the desires of our hearts, too. I believe that He is a loving God that would like for us to achieve our desires as long as they match up to His will for us. He also wants us to be obedient to Him first.

What are your desires for your future? What is it that God has called you to do for Him? This isn't a prosperity message, but what if achieving the first question involved you doing the second one first? God could do that.

Personal Greetings
Romans 16: 1-27

This is the last chapter of the Book of Romans and it appears to be a lengthy end of a letter. For a second, I thought I was reading a New Testament version of 'the begats'. There's a bunch of people Paul is thanking and giving a 'shout out' to. I guess he could have made it simple by saying, "Thank y'all!", but he didn't. I wonder why.

If you look at the names of the people that he mentions, you'll see some important people that helped him in ministry and some that made a difference in his life. He went the extra step and included some information as to why he considered them so important. That's pretty cool!

It's interesting to me that many women were mentioned and Paul gave them respect by including them in these verses. Many churches out there tend to put women at the bottom of their status ladder. Some won't let women minister at all. But, Paul shows us that women are just as important as men when it comes to serving God. Paul gives them credit for their efforts because he knows that these women ministered to him. That's awesome to know.

I guess the main lesson from these verses is that a ministry consists of a team of people working together for the same goals. We may have thought of Paul as a solo act that went out into the world by himself doing all these great things, but he wasn't. He had help. God provided him with the people he needed to get the job done and Paul recognized that.

Many people today are scared to step out on faith to do what God has called them to do. They may see themselves as a one-person ministry with the big job of taking on the world. That's scary! But, it ain't going to be like that. God just wants us to step out on faith. He will provide the people, the tools, and anything we need to serve Him in the job He has for us.

Ladies, you have a big purpose in ministry, too. It's not just for men. You are important! Don't let anyone tell you otherwise.

Paul ends his letter telling us to watch out. There will be some that will try to cause division and teach us things that are different than what God's Word tells us. Watch out! Our protection against this is to always seek God's Word ourselves. This means to read the Bible and pray for the Holy Spirit to tell you what He wants you to know from it. Compare for yourself what others tell you with what God says in His Word.

When we go to church, don't just sit and listen. Let's bring our Bibles and compare notes. We can't just assume that what the preacher says is true. Preachers are human too and will make mistakes. We will never know what God's Word says until we really read it ourselves. Ya know?

The Book Of
1st Corinthians

The Book Of 1ˢᵗ Corinthians

Introduction To 1ˢᵗ Corinthians

1 Corinthians, as we already know is one of the many books in

the Bible that were written by the Apostle Paul. It's basically a letter inspired by God to a church located in a place called Corinth. I have never been there personally and couldn't tell you where all the hot spots were or even if they had a local Wally World, but Paul was familiar with the place and the people that lived there. He had been there before and shared the Gospel with them. He helped start the church during one of his missionary journeys.

This letter that Paul wrote them was intended to help them with some issues they were having. You see, they were Christians living in an environment of sin. They had all kinds of junk going on around them. Some were trying to adapt with their environment and this affected the church.

1 Corinthians was written around A.D. 55. Paul addresses issues such as unity (not division) among the people, how they should grow in their faith, dealing with immorality and lawsuits among Christians, church discipline, a woman's role in the church, worship, spiritual gifts, and he even talks about sex. This could be interesting. Grab your Bible and dig in with me. Let's see what we can get from it. Who knows? We might learn something.

Division in Corinth
1 Corinthians 1: 1-17

Undoubtedly Paul received some reports that the church in Corinth was having some issues. Can you imagine following God's leading in your life to start something for Him (a church or ministry), and then when you walk away to do something else for the Lord, you learn through reliable sources that the other thing you started was falling apart. I imagine it could be a little stressful. You would hope it could take care of itself, so that you could move on to something else. But no! You have to go back to it and fix it! It would make you feel like a babysitter as it pulls you back from going forward in life.

Paul was placed in a leadership position by God to direct His people. He wanted to keep them encouraged and strong in their faith. It was a tough job, but God gave him everything he needed to do it and undoubtedly felt he was the man for the job. Satan was also alive and well back in those days as he is today and we all know how he loves to stir up trouble. Right? Well, he was doing a number on the church in Corinth. One of his cool tricks was to cause division in the church.

When I speak of division in a church, I'm not talking about putting men on the left side and women on the right. It's not about putting the kids in one building and the grownups in another. Oh no! Satan was creating problems that made the church people believe in different things. Paul wanted the Christians to be in one mind and one accord. This is the same thing that Jesus taught.

When I read this, I can't help but think of the different religions in the world today. And after you separate them and focus on the ones that fall under the Christian category, it separates even further. You have Baptists, Methodists, Catholics, and many others. And even after you separate these, it breaks down into more. For example, how many types of Baptist churches are out there? There's quite a bit. The sad thing is that as years pass by, it will keep on dividing. Jesus wasn't about all this. He's about one mind and one accord. Paul was sharing this information with the church at Corinth and it still applies to us today.

If you put a wolf in a sheep pen, the first thing he will do is separate the sheep. He will cause them to scatter. He then looks for the weak one and then jumps on it. Satan is like a wolf and has been playing the division game for quite some time. It's important for everyone to get into God's Word and read it for ourselves so that we can all be in one mind and one accord. As preachers and teachers speak, compare what they are saying with what is in the Bible. Don't just take their word for it! They are human and could be giving some false information. It's best to know for sure by checking for ourselves. As Christians, we are followers of Jesus, not preachers! Remember that!

Christ the Wisdom and Power of God
1 Corinthians 1: 18 – 2: 5

Everything about Jesus' appearance and message was simple. He was a simple man with a simple plan to save the world. The folks back then were expecting a Messiah, a savior, to come and save them from their troubles and had a picture in their mind of a powerful king all decked out in fancy clothes, carrying weapons of mass destruction while riding in a chariot pulled by stampeding horses, and spoke words of power and wisdom. But, what they got was a poor carpenter's kid. I don't think He was what they were expecting, so they crucified Him.

The message of the cross packs a lot of power. This is where Jesus died as a living sacrifice for the sins of the world. This act built a bridge that connected all of humanity back to God to those that believe in Jesus. But, many folks don't get it and may think of it as foolish. But, to those of us that are saved, we understand the importance of it and know that if Jesus didn't die on the cross, we would all be in a mess. That's the power of the cross!

If people understood where they stood before Almighty God — lost in sin and separated from Him - they would think differently. The problem we have in this world is that many think they know it all and are in charge of their own destiny. We seek knowledge and wisdom as if it is the power that sustains us. But, it's not. We are specks of sand on this big planet. Satan fills a lot of people's head with ignorance in thinking that because of their 'smarts' or 'high position' in life that they've got it going on. This superior feeling makes many people think that they don't need God, but they're wrong. We all need God!

I believe the key here is knowing that God can use anybody, but we have to be willing to let Him. Actually, if you read in the Bible of the people He chose for certain jobs, you'll see that many of them were regular ordinary folks that were obedient to His call on their life. You had anyone from simple fishermen to simple sheep herders. But, you also had some with authority. They all had one thing in common. They knew that without God leading them, they were nothing. If they did something cool for God, they knew they couldn't take credit for it. It was all Him.

Wisdom from the Spirit
1 Corinthians 2: 6 – 16

After reading these verses, you start thinking, "Whoa! That was deep! What was that all about?" I know because I just felt the same way after I read it.

What is this wisdom that Christian people get that others don't understand? Why is it such a mystery and hidden anyway? What is Paul talking about?

At first glance, you would think that being a Christian qualifies you to receive super human powers. This could include having the ability to leap tall buildings with a single bound, fly faster than a speeding bullet or simply have cool spider senses that help you to know when something bad is going to happen. But, so far I haven't had any of those abilities and I know without a doubt that I'm a Christian. So, what's up?

As we already know, Paul is writing a letter to the church in Corinth. These folks were pretty smart and maybe high in social status. I would bet they were very educated and knew a thing or two about everything. They knew the Laws of Moses up and down and left and right. I'm sure many of them could even recite it. Based on those laws, they knew the steps of what to do to make things right in the sight of God. They could kill a few farm animals to receive forgiveness for their sins and even do some of the other things mentioned in those laws to make life just peachy. But, Paul was sharing something new with them. He was preaching about Jesus – His death and resurrection. Paul wanted them to know that the only way to make things right before God was to ask for forgiveness and to accept Jesus Christ as their Lord and Savior and to believe on Him. They thought this way of thinking was weird. To them, it just didn't make any sense. Jesus, to them, was just that carpenter's trouble-making kid that they crucified some time ago.

Even today, people don't fully understand the Gospel. Folks will say, "As soon as I start living right, I'll get saved." They make it seem as if they need to clean their life up first before accepting Jesus into their life. The truth is, they need Jesus in their life first in order to clean their life up. People find it hard to believe that God would provide such a simple plan for Salvation, but He has. We make it too complicated when it wasn't originally intended to be.

The way God works in people's lives doesn't make sense to us. Or at least it doesn't from a natural human standpoint. He does things in a way that leaves people amazed. He puts us into situations where we have to totally depend on Him and His provision, while the people that are watching us look at us and think we are totally stupid for practicing that kind of faith. This whole faith thing doesn't make sense in their eyes. To them, it's like we're walking on thin ice with our life in the balance, and instead of us taking action in trying to solve our own problems, we're trusting in God. And when they see Him come through in our times of need, they don't know what to say. That's a mystery!

As Christ-followers, we have the Holy Spirit within us, guiding our lives and directing our paths. God uses us for His work here on Earth to share Him and His message with the world. The cool thing is that God will give us the right words to say in certain situations. He may put us in places where we may meet someone that needed to hear something from God. Those words that come from our mouths will be exactly what they needed and they will probably feel awkward that it came from us.

Have you ever heard of divine appointment? This is when you just so happen to be going somewhere and you just so happen to meet someone that presents to you with that thing you needed. It could be a word or a material thing, but you knew it was weird timing that you met them. That's God working it all out.

Have you ever prayed for something to happen and a spiritual door opened up and you knew that it was opened for you by God? Or how about this, have you ever had a door open up and you felt a sense of something not being right and you knew that you weren't supposed to enter? This whole process is called spiritual discernment. It's when the Holy Spirit tells you what is of God and what isn't. It's more of a feeling inside that will either bring you peace or a sense of dread. This is how God directs your path in life.

God's ways are weird and goes against the way we, as human beings, would do things. God's wisdom is a mystery to folks that don't know Him. As we grow as Christians, God will give us opportunities every day to know Him better. Just know that everything He does in our life is to bring us closer to Him and to help mold us to be more like Jesus.

On Divisions of the Church
1 Corinthians 3: 1-23

The thing that caught my eye was that Paul was talking to Christians that weren't growing in their faith. Actually, the real problem was where they had put their faith. It wasn't in Jesus, but in the ministers and preachers.

From the scripture, it seems as though they were followers of the

men presenting God's Word. It tells us that some were saying they were of Apollos and others of Paul. That's not how it works! What about Jesus? These guys were just pieces in the big puzzle that spiritually worked together for the same purpose – leading others to Him. The people Paul was talking to were followers of man.

Many churches today are guilty of this. Some look to the preacher as The All-Knowing - The Man With The Plan. Some model their lives according to how he does things , how he lives, and by what he says. Stop! No!! A preacher is just a man! He will make mistakes! They are not perfect and are sinners just like everybody else on this planet. We should focus on Jesus and see the preachers out there as messengers – spiritual mail carriers. Better yet, we should check out their spiritual mail that they give us and compare it to God's Word to see if it's not junk mail. You know what I'm saying? That's a good message right there!

Paul also shares with us how it's important to work together in ministry. Each one of us has a special purpose and should do our part. Here again, it's like a puzzle and we are all a piece of it. Someone may share the Gospel with someone, while somebody else prays for them, and a few days down the road, someone actually leads them to the Lord. That's three pieces of the puzzle working together for the same cause. Pretty cool, huh?

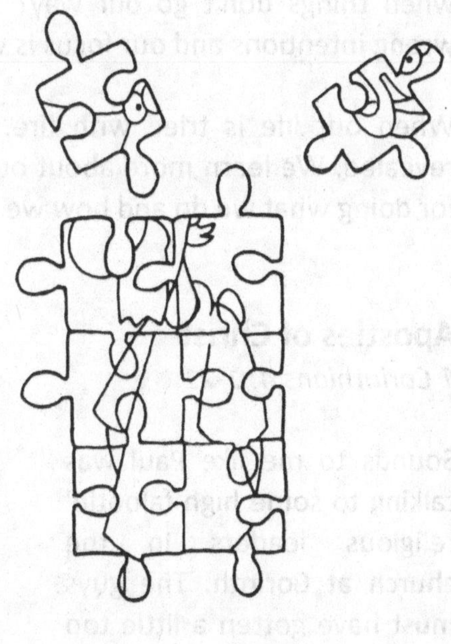

Let's say that the first person didn't share the Gospel with them. This person refused to do it because they had better things to do. Now God will have to fill their space with someone else to do it for them and they will have to give account to why they were disobedient. Not good!

Paul told the church that he laid the foundation for them to build on - Jesus. He wanted them to be cautious of what they build with because it would be tested with fire. I believe that is why Christians go through some rough times. It's during those times when we show what we are made of. Are we truly who we say we are? Are we trusting? Do we really believe what the Bible says?

The same is true in ministry. Are we really focused on Jesus by sharing the Gospel with someone? Or do we get our feelings hurt when things don't go our way? It could be that we have the wrong intentions and our focus is wrong.

When our life is tried with fire, it's amazing of what can be revealed. We learn more about ourselves and our inner purpose for doing what we do and how we act.

Apostles of Christ
1 Corinthians 4: 1-21

Sounds to me like Paul was talking to some high falootin' religious leaders in the church at Corinth. The guys must have gotten a little too big for their britches and felt they knew it all and were quick to judge people that didn't.

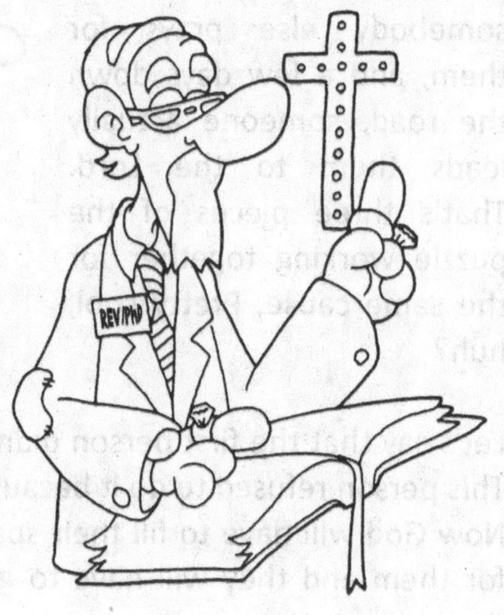

Paul reminded them that we are all servants of Christ and that we should humble ourselves when it comes to sharing 'Jesus stuff' with others. We should take the job seriously and be faithful in doing everything that God has called us to do.

As Christians in leadership positions, we are no better than anyone else. God has placed us where He wants us, not to look down on other people, but to serve them out of obedience to Him. We shouldn't judge folks! It's hard to lead others to Jesus when your finger is pointing in the opposite direction of the cross. Ouch!

We should approach people in need with love and understanding. For those people needing Jesus in their life, we shouldn't judge them and point out all of their reasons why they need Him. Telling them that they are a rotten, messed up pile of poo-poo is not going to open their hearts to Jesus. If anything, it will harden it. Just be understanding to their problems, let them know they need Him and then show them the way to receive Him. I hope that made sense.

Paul was trying to lead by example. He wanted them to follow his way of doing things because he was following Jesus. These church leaders had gotten all puffed up like a bag of Cheetos and forgot all about Jesus and their real purpose for doing what they do.

They were living the big life while Paul was starving to death and homeless. Not that being broke is a sign of holiness, but these guys may have turned their ministry opportunity into a lucrative religious business. Who knows?

The one thing we all can be sure of is that God knows our hearts. He knows our motives for doing things. Yes, we may be doing all kinds of cool Christian stuff, but where is our heart at when we do them? Is it on Jesus? Are we earnestly trying to serve others and lead them to Him? Or maybe we're thinking more on ourselves and what we can get from it.

Expel the Immoral Brother
1 Corinthians 5: 1-13

This is about sin in the church. And from the sounds of it, this may have been one of those churches whose members' family tree didn't have any branches. Sons were having sex with their

Mothers. Eww!

If you're wondering what could possibly be the wrong with that, then you may want to get your life right. It's sexually immoral! Plus, it's gross! That's your Mama and you shouldn't be dating her. Just sayin'.

Undoubtedly this type of thing was going on in the church at Corinth. They were just letting it happen and acting like it was no big deal. I imagine this fella was an outstanding church member and probably taught Sunday school. He may have been the Choir Director. Who knows? The people may have seen all of the good stuff that he contributed to the church and overlooked that small insignificant detail of his life. What would it have hurt?

Paul says the sin would work its way through the church and mess everybody up. The next thing you know the whole congregation would look like a Gigolo Convention singing church hymns. That's why Paul told them to kick him out. That junk doesn't belong in church. Now Paul wasn't telling them that they couldn't hang out with them out in the world because that's how you reach the lost with the Gospel. He just didn't want them to be part of the church.

He goes on to say that church membership should not consist of the following type of people:

- fornicator (sexual immoral)
- covetous (greedy)
- idolaters
- railer (slanderers)
- drunkards
- extortioner (swindlers)

Many churches today would probably lose a lot of memberships and dollars, but Paul says, "Kick 'em out!"

Lawsuits Among Believers
1 Corinthians 6: 1-11

Some Christians refuse to take others to court with lawsuits because of this scripture right here. Many read it as saying to never go before a judge. I read it a little differently.

Paul is talking to the church. Undoubtedly, the members had some issues going on with each other and instead of working together to solve their problems, they took it to their local court system.

Paul felt that they, as Christians, should be able to work out their problems. By getting the church involved, everyone could work up a solution based on God's Word, prayer, and experiences from other believers. That would make more sense.

Paul also realized the purpose of the church as 'being a light in the world'. If two Christians were to appear in court with their problems and got all 'Jerry Springer' up in front of people that needed Jesus in their life, it would have chased them away. Who would want to be a Christian if it meant being like those two clowns? I mean...c'mon!

How does that apply to us today? Should Christians ever go to court? I believe Christian people should try and resolve their problems among themselves. We should make things right with each other. If someone does us wrong, we should confront them and allow them to either justify actions or simply make it right.

The fact is that people are watching our lives and they're taking notes. Our lives should reflect Jesus. If they see drama in our life all the time, they're not going to want any of it. I believe that was the main point Paul was trying to get across to the church in Corinth.

In today's world, there are going to be issues that people can't resolve on their own. In some cases they will have to go to court. This is usually because both people can't agree on a solution or that one person wants to be hard-headed.

For the Christian, after they have tried to work it out, they will have to make a choice. Is the issue worth the time and energy to go before a judge? Or is it so minor that you can just turn the other cheek?

Sexual Immorality
1 Corinthians 6: 12-20

These verses get used by a lot of religious people, especially when they are wanting to tell others all of the things they are doing wrong in their life.

To me, these verses are more about sexual junk that we shouldn't be doing because it goes against God's original plans He had for man and woman.

First let's talk about the verse that gets recited the most:

What? know ye not that your body is the temple of the Holy Ghost [which is] in you, which ye have of God, and ye are not your own? - 1 Corinthians 6: 19

It is true that our body is the temple of God. If you read the verses before it, the main subject is about sexual relations.

Religious people will tell you that smoking cigarettes is a sin and then they quote this verse. They will say that drinking alcohol is a sin and back it with this verse. I know this will be a touchy subject, but I don't see how it relates.

If religious people were so concerned about putting harmful stuff in their bodies, every Christian out there would be healthy athletes. They definitely wouldn't be first in line at the all-you-can-eat buffet dinners on Sunday afternoon. Know what I mean?

Paul says in verse 12 that everything is lawful, but not expedient. The NIV version says, "everything is permissible, but not beneficial". This tells me that we can put whatever we want to into our bodies, even though it may not be good for us.

Smoking cigarettes is bad for your health, but it doesn't make you a bad person nor separate you from God. Drinking alcohol in small amounts won't put you in the lake of fire. Actually, in the scriptures it says its good for the stomach.

Let me also add, drinking it in excess will make you a drunk and God has some issues with that because it alters our mental state. We need to be able to think clearly especially if we have leadership positions such as being the role models in our homes.

Paul was basically saying that he could put whatever he wanted into his body, but he didn't want to be controlled by it. My thinking would be that we shouldn't get ourselves to the point that we can't function without eating or drinking that 'thing' every day before we get out of the house. That would be considered an addiction and that's probably something we should get rid of.

Paul was talking about sex – the bad kind. God designed man and woman. He created marriage to join the couple together like super glue. He also created sex for them to have kids and for recreational fun. All of this was by God's design and He is cool about it.

Now here's where it gets weird. Sex was intended to be a spiritual thing between a married couple in the sight of God. Well, the next thing you know, it turns into people sleeping with whoever or whatever they want. This messes up the spiritual plan and it comes with a terrible price. Check the stats on divorce rates in America. Look at the various sexually transmitted diseases floating around. Take a peek at how many kids out there that are suffering because their Mom and Dad are no longer together.

I could go on and on with this topic. These verses are about immoral sex, not about eating foods high in cholesterol.

Instruction On Christian Marriage
1 Corinthians 7: 1-40

Paul was single and had never been married. He was totally souled-out to the Lord. He didn't want his relationship with Him to be hindered with the stuff that husbands go through by trying to keep a wife happy. I mean, we go through a lot of stuff. Right fellas?

I guess Paul realized by watching his Christian buddies that they had to spend a lot of time with their soul mates. I'm sure Paul asked some of them on occasions to hang out and talk about Jesus stuff with him, but they may have refused 'cause their wives had made other plans for them to either go shopping or watch a romantic comedy movie with them on Camel TV or something.

As married Christians, we have to divide our time up. Jesus is number one and spouse is number two, but we realize the importance of keeping a balance. If we devote too much time on the Lord, we may be neglecting our family duties. Paul knew this and chose to live the single life and give the Lord and his ministry 100%.

One of the major problems back in the day when this letter was written to the church was sexual immorality. It seems people were tempted to do all kinds of weird sexual stuff. I can't and don't want to imagine the kind of junk that went on back then, but it was pretty serious. Even though Paul thought it would be cool if folks didn't get married, he felt that marriage would help those that were getting tempted by the sexual weirdness.

In marriage, it should be one man for one woman and each should work together as a team to strengthen this physical bond they have. They now have become one. Spiritually, as Christians, we belong to God. Physically, we belong to our spouses.

One of the things that stood out to me is from verse 5. It talks about how we should not deprive our spouses except by mutual consent and for a time so that we can devote ourselves to prayer. To me, this is talking about sex. As wives and husbands, we can't use our role as a sexual partner against our spouses by holding back or using it as a tool to get what we want from them. This verse is more of an encouragement to married couples to keep the bedroom busy so that neither partner gets tempted by the weird sexual stuff out there.

Marriage is a sanctified God thing. He set it up and was meant to be a blessing for man and woman. But, because folks stopped following God's Word concerning marriage and forgot how He wanted us to treat each other, divorce has become a common word. God doesn't like divorce.

Paul offers advice to those that are unequally yoked – Christians married to un-Christians. He says it's best to stay together. Life is too short and we shouldn't trouble ourselves about it and try to make the best of it. Who knows? That lost loved one may see Jesus in you and want some, too.

Food Sacrificed To Idols
1 Corinthians 8: 1-13

The folks at Corinth had a dilemma. They knew that some of the meat products being sold at the local marketplace may have been offered as a sacrifice to idols. They didn't want to eat something that was part of some kind of pagan ceremony in fear that the 'poo' of idolatry might get on them.

It's true that people would

sacrifice animals at their pagan temples. I'm sure the chief priests figured out a way to earn an income from the meat that would be wasted. They may have offered a deal to the local butcher who had a shop downtown. He might of taken the meat and sliced it up into deli sandwich slices and used the fatty chunks for potted meat and sausage links. Who knows? The people that came into his store wouldn't know for sure if the meat offered came from the pagan temple or if it met idolatry-free meat standards. I'm sure the meat wasn't marked with a stamp. It was risky.

Paul set the people straight by sharing some cool information. Yes, people have knowledge and if they put a little brain power into the situation, they could determine which meats in the market came from the pagan temple. They could figure it out. They could do the math and the detective work and learn all kinds of stuff about the food they put in their body and where it comes from. And then they could decide whether to eat it or not.

But those that love God, He knows their hearts and the purpose behind the things they do. A person eating pagan meat without knowledge of where it came from could eat it freely without feeling guilty. The same is true today, we don't have to spend a lot of time trying to figure out if something we do stems from some kind of pagan ritual. If our conscience is clear and we aren't worshiping idols when we do stuff, we shouldn't worry about it.

A thought that comes to mind is the holiday seasons we celebrate — Christmas, Easter, Halloween, and the Jolly Redneck Festival. It seems like every one of them can somehow be traced back to some kind of pagan ceremony. We may celebrate them because they're fun and innocent and could honestly care less about where they came from, but some people make it a big deal. They won't celebrate the holiday.

I've known people to quit using a certain brand toothpaste because they heard the manufacturer was in a satanic cult. They said their hygiene products displayed a wicked symbol on it that could be linked back to the cult. The news about it spread like

FULL SPEED AHEAD!! MY SUPER COOL TOOTHPASTE WILL MAKE EVERYONE BOW DOWN TO ME! BW AHAHAHA!

wildfire and told Christians everywhere that they should throw the stuff away if they had it in their homes.

But ya know, using toothpaste or celebrating holidays doesn't bring us closer or take us away from God as long as we're not in it for the pagan stuff. Does that make sense? I mean, when you're brushing your teeth, are you focused on worshiping Satan by doing it? I doubt it! You're probably like me, you just want to get your teeth clean. And how about Halloween? Do you celebrate it because you know it's the cool pagan thing to do? Or is it for the big bag of candy?

There is freedom in being a Christian because we are not saved by our deeds or by following rules. It's a free gift from God. However, we have to be careful how we practice our freedom. There are Christians out there that could be offended by our actions. Even if something is cool with us, we have to look out for our brothers and sisters in Christ. It may mean not doing some things in their presence to keep them from falling. I believe that is what Paul was telling them in Corinth.

The Rights of an Apostle
1 Corinthians 9: 1-27

I guess some of the folks at Corinth questioned Paul's credentials as an Apostle. He was being judged. Imagine that.

There will be many times in our Christian walk when people will judge us and point fingers. In some cases they may be right. It's during those times that we have to step back and take a look at our own life. Instead of getting offended, we could take a moment to evaluate ourselves and see how the way we are living compares to what God's Word says.

The thing we can learn from these verses is that, when we are truly living the Christian lifestyle, lives around us are going to change and people are going to take notice. Our faith will have an impact on somebody. We should pray that God will use us to be more effective in His work here on Earth.

The people that were judging Paul were the same people that his life touched. Their new life was a result of his obedience to God in sharing the Gospel with them. It seems he had to remind them of it.

These folks at Corinth were giving Paul a hard time. They should have been glad to see him and should've welcomed him into the church and in their homes. They could have given him a fluffy chair and asked him if there was anything he needed. Paul was a traveling preacher sharing the Gospel and had a very important job working for the Lord, but they didn't seem to care.

As an Apostle, he had rights. In addition to the right of receiving warm welcomes from his Christian brothers and sisters, he also had the right to be married and to be paid for his work.

Paid? I know that sounds a little weird because we automatically think preachers and ministers should be self-maintained. I mean, they work directly for the Lord and we would assume they get Heavenly paychecks signed and delivered directly from Jesus. Why should we, as a church and individually, pay them? We're already having a hard time giving our church our offerings every week. Right?

But, the fact is, the Lord commanded that those that preach the Gospel should receive their living from the Gospel. Churches should pay those that work in the church. Do a study on the pay scale for that position and pay them for it. That's what it's telling me.

Here's what happens if we don't pay those that preach the Gospel. People need money to provide for their families. Ministry work takes time that could be used in working a regular 9-to-5 job that actually pays with cash instead of 'pats on the back'. Economically speaking, a person will go broke sharing God's Word with others if we don't pay them or they will be forced to stop doing what God has told them to do. It will be our fault because we have failed to obey God's command. You see what I'm saying? We need to pay these folks.

I guess Paul had an issue with tight-wadded people. He didn't want to hinder his preaching and God's Word by asking anybody for money. I can understand his way of thinking. I remember years ago when I was in a singing ministry. Churches would invite us to sing to their congregation. It was an honor

and a privilege. It gave us an opportunity to share the Gospel and offer hope to those in need. However, we were broke and wondered who would pick up the gas tab to get us there. In many cases the preacher would automatically pass around an offering plate for us because we never had the guts to ask. It's hard to sing about Jesus with a tip jar in your hand. People should just know to offer it without being asked.

Paul was a free man and wasn't bound to no one except God. However, in his ministry, he chose to be a slave to everyone with the hopes of leading them to Jesus. He would fit himself into their environment. If they were Jews, he would live like a Jew when he was around them. The same applied to those under the law and to those without the law. Paul was like a chameleon that changed colors in its environment.

If I had to relate this to today's world, I believe if Paul knew he was preaching to a group of bikers, he would probably be wearing a leather vest and pull up on a motorcycle. If he were preaching to gangstas on the Eastside, he would probably have his baggy clothes on with a doo-rag around his head. Paul was serious about sharing the Gospel with everyone and knew that in order for them to listen to him, he had to be like them. We could learn something from this and apply it to our lives and ministry.

Can you imagine a goody-goody shoeshine preacher trying to preach to a bunch of hillbilly rednecks? They would probably throw him in the lake. You see what I'm saying? Paul was about fitting in with the crowd to make his ministry more effective. To me, that makes sense. How about you?

Warnings from Israel's History
1 Corinthians 10: 1-13

Paul used an illustration from Israel's history, back when Moses led them out of Egypt to the Promised Land. Remember that one? It was a journey that has so many life lessons that can be applied to us.

Paul mentions four details from the Old Testament and warns the church at Corinth:

Don't be idolaters (Exodus 32)
The Israelites built a golden calf in the middle of the desert and began worshiping it. Sounds kinda silly don't it? I mean, they were following Moses and saw all the cool things God had done for them, and then out of the blue, they build a golden calf.

But, you know, how many times have we turned from a relationship with God to a life filled with other things? We know God is real and He has done many miraculous things in our life, but for some reason we get preoccupied and turn our backs on Him. We quit reading the Bible, praying, and going to church. You know the drill and I have been guilty of it many times myself.

We built a golden calf. It's time to tear it down and get serious with the Lord.

Don't be committing sexual immorality
(Numbers 25: 1-9)
Sexual immorality has always been a problem in society. It goes against God and His way of life for us and He doesn't like it.

Many of the Israelites got involved with some sexual junk with the Moabite women, who were probably prostitutes. The result ended with 23,000 dying in one day. That's pretty serious!

What is sexual immorality? The Bible gives us some information on this topic. Here are some scriptures:

Adultery – Exodus 20:14
"Thou shalt not commit adultery."

That's pretty plain and simple. It's one of the Ten Commandments. It's when you mess around with someone's spouse. It's not cool!

Not only is God against it, but I'm sure that spouse's husband or wife wouldn't appreciate it too much either. Breaking this commandment could make them break one, too. Ya know, the one about killing. It's the verse before this one.

Fornication – Hebrews 13:4
"Marriage is honourable in all, and the bed undefiled: but whoremongers and adulterers God will judge."

God put marriage together. That's His deal! It was meant for man and woman. Sex comes after marriage – not before. I imagine that comes as a shock in today's society. Actually, being sexually active with as many people as possible is acceptable. But, not to God.

Sexual perversions – Leviticus 18:6
"None of you shall approach to any that is near of kin to him, to uncover their nakedness: I am the LORD."

To be fooling around with your first cousin falls into this category. It's not a good thing! It doesn't even matter if you marry her.

There are other sexual acts that are considered perverted, but hopefully you get the idea.

Immorality of the mind – Matthew 5:28
"But I say unto you, That whosoever looketh on a woman to lust after her hath committed adultery with her already in his heart."

There's a lot of sexual stuff to look at around us. It's on TV – on movies, TV shows, and in advertising. It's in magazines and all over the internet. Sex sells and it gets our attention.

We have to learn and train ourselves to just look away. That junk burns a photographic image in our minds and it's hard to get it out of there.

Don't be testing the Lord (Numbers 21: 5, 6)
Testing the Lord from this scripture refers to how the Israelites acted when they didn't get the things they wanted. They became impatient and spoke against God.

I believe God sometimes makes us wait for His answer to our prayers to see how we will act during the waiting process. You can learn a lot about your faith in God and about your character as a Christian when you're in the waiting line.

I know from personal experience that I have been mad at God for not answering my prayers when I wanted them answered. I have stopped serving Him a few times because He didn't respond to a need I had on my schedule. My negative reaction was testing God.

For the Israelites, God sent

some poisonous snakes and they killed a few of them.

Don't be grumbling (Numbers 14: 2, 36; 16: 41-50)
Grumbling is when we start to focus on the things we don't have, instead of being thankful for what we do have. Just like the people of Israel did, we forget what God has already done for us and that He is working on things ahead of us, too. He has a plan set in motion and is teaching and growing us through life lessons. The worst thing we can do is grumble. Let His perfect work do its thing. He's in control.
The Israelite's grumbling cost them thousands of lives.

Knowing that I have been guilty of a few of these things listed against God makes me very thankful for His mercy on me. We should all take these warnings from Paul very seriously. If we are guilty, we should make every effort to make things right. God is Almighty and we are small specks of sand compared to His greatness.

Paul ends these verses with some hope. God is faithful and knows that these temptations are common to man. We will be faced with decisions to either give in to them or run. God makes us a promise that He will not allow us to be tempted more than we bear without His help. He will provide us a way out. It's our choice to take that exit.

Idol Feasts and the Lord's Supper
1 Corinthians 10: 14-22

The Corinthians were dabbling in some cultic activity. They were sharing the feast ceremony table with folks that worshiped idols. Were they just trying to get a free meal? According to Paul, I don't think so.

It was as if they were taking part of the Lord's Supper by breaking bread with their Christian brothers and sisters and then heading over to the pagan temple to celebrate with them, too. Paul told them that you can't do both.

This would be a message to Christians who try and live double lives. These folks do the Jesus-thing once a week and basically live the way they want for the remainder of the week. As Christians, we have guidelines that God has given us to follow. It's all right there in the Bible. We should be following Jesus.

Another message would be about idols. I know it may seem farfetched, but idols are present in the world today just like they were back in Paul's day. They used to be made from stone and wood and carved into statues for worship. Now they are being made more economically from plastic and paper – and turned into credit cards and cash. Knowing where we put our trust could determine who or what our idols are in our life.

The Believer's Freedom
1 Corinthians 10: 23-33, 11: 1

Some of us spend a great deal of time trying to make a list of the 'rights and wrongs' of Christian living. In some cases, people find wrong in just about everything in life and make being a Christian dull and boring. The sad thing is when they begin to preach their convictions to others and expect them to follow their guidelines. To me, this just ain't right.

The day we accepted Jesus into our life and got saved, it was because we became convicted of our sins and knew we needed forgiveness. The Holy Spirit stepped in and began working in us. Right?

The Bible is our tool to discover how God wants us to live and we should follow its instructions to become more like Jesus. It's a lifelong process of growing. And, when it's done right, this new life will begin affecting those around us in a positive way. They are going to want this life, too.

If we walk through this life finding wrong in everything, it makes us look bad. Nobody wants a life like this. We will not be an effective witness for the Lord. If anything, we become the reason why someone wouldn't want to be a Christian. And that's not a good thing!

I believe if the Bible doesn't specify something is wrong, then it must be OK. The Ten Commandments says killing is wrong, then don't kill somebody. Chewing gum on Sunday is OK because the Bible doesn't say any different. You see where I'm getting at with this? Allow the Holy Spirit to convict our hearts of the things we should and shouldn't do and it will match what's in the Bible.

We can't live a Christian life in fear. We are to live a life that glorifies God. This would mean following what is spelled out to us in His Word, not from what other people say is wrong. We have freedom.

Keep in mind, there are going to be others out there that may feel wrong about doing certain things that we're OK with. We should respect their convictions and not do those things around them. In all that we do, we should glorify God and look out for the best of others. This is the servant attitude that Jesus had and the one we should have, too.

Propriety in Worship
1 Corinthians 11: 2-16

At first glance, it appears that it is wrong for women to cut their hair and to not wear ball caps. For the fellas, it makes you think that they should never wear a ball cap at all. For a simple man, this could create a problem. And to top it all off, it seems the man should be bossing the wife around because he's the Big Chief in the family. Wow! You could almost start a new religion with these scriptures.

I think there's more to these scriptures than what it first appears. Keep in mind, we are dealing with a church at Corinth and a culture from around A.D. 55. I'm sure things were different than what they are today. I know in my lifetime, the culture has changed at least a few times. My kids remind me of it every time I pull a shirt out of my closet. My choice of fashion is based on the culture I grew up in years ago.

The scripture here, to me, is about church unity. Paul was addressing issues in the church at Corinth that was causing division. He wanted everyone to work together. It may have been part of the culture in those days for men to pray without a hat on and women to pray with a hat on. Who knows? But, if it was part of the 'praying scene' back then and people didn't follow the rules, it would probably hinder someone else in the church. It would show disrespect to others and maybe mess them up when they prayed.

These scriptures have always been used in present time to point fingers at others when it comes to hair. If a man comes to church with long hair, he might get escorted out the door. To me, this is wrong judgment. Long hair in society is acceptable and should be acceptable in church. The same applies to women that want to

119

sport out short hair. Who cares? There are a lot of lost people out there that need to come to church. We should invite them all to come in, regardless of how long their hair is.

In my opinion, maybe the folks that come to church with the big fluffy hair should get special seating arrangements on the back pew. This way we can still see the choir when they sing. I mean, that's just my own thoughts on the subject.

The Lord's Supper
1 Corinthians 11: 17-34

The Lord's Supper is a serious deal. It's a reminder to us of Jesus' death and our hope of His return. We strengthen our faith because, by doing it, we're having fellowship with Jesus and since we're doing this with other believers, we strengthen ourselves as a church.

So, what's so cool about eating a dry cracker and small cup of grape juice? It goes back to Luke 22: 13-20, Jesus is having a Passover meal with His disciples. They're eating from a table of food, probably similar to what we would eat on Thanksgiving at a relative's home. The next thing you know, Jesus shares with them some wine and bread. He informs them that by eating the bread, it represents His body. The wine, it represents His blood. And then He says, "Do this in remembrance of Me."

I believe He was talking to them as a church, a unit of believers, to take time to remember Him. The crackers and grape juice symbolizes what Jesus did with His disciples. When we do this, our focus should be on all that Jesus did for us that led Him to the cross. We should remember His death and how He delivered us from sin. It should be a Jesus-moment.

However, from the scriptures, the church at Corinth turned it into a gluttonous all-you-can-eat-and-drink fest. Paul wasn't happy about it. He reminded them of what the Lord's Supper was all about and how serious it was.

We should take it seriously, too.

Spiritual Gifts
1 Corinthians 12: 1-11

God gives each of us spiritual gifts to serve Him and to use when leading others to Him. We're all on the same team using our gifts for the same purpose and goal. We shouldn't be competing.

A thought that comes to my mind is in the music ministry. These people are gifted with the talent to sing and play musical instruments. They use their gifts to sing praises to God. Many join forces with other members and start a Christian music group. It's a great ministry and music makes an impact on people's lives.

The problem is when the musicians forget why they do what they do. They may focus more on their fan list and how many of them come to their shows. By making changes in what God has gifted them with in order to bring in more crowds may affect the spiritual purpose the group was designed to do.

Some may even compete with other Christian groups in a battle-of-the-bands type of competition to see who's the best. I mean, it's all fun and all, but we shouldn't try to compete with others to see who's better in ministry. We are really all part of the same team and each of us have different assignments. One group may be together to reach only certain people while another group is designed to reach millions. Who knows?

Even though our gifts may be different than one another, they work together like pieces of a puzzle. The Holy Spirit directs our gifts when we allow Him to have control and use us. We should also be content with what God has given us to work with.

One Body, Many Parts
1 Corinthians 12: 12-31

Paul uses these verses to describe how the body of Christ should work together just like the human body.

If you think really hard about how complex the human body is, you would soon realize how many parts we're actually working with. It's more than just arms and legs, a head, and a big ol' belly. There are small parts inside with big names that I can't pronounce. But the cool thing is how it all works together to put the body in motion.

Think about the heart for a minute. It's a small organ with a big job. It keeps the body alive by pumping blood to all of the other organs. What if it stopped doing it's job? Now think of all the tiny veins that are all over the place. What if a few of them decided to take a break and close up shop. The blood wouldn't flow to where it needed to go. This could cause some serious problems and affect the body.

The body of Christ is the same way. As Christians, we are part of that body and are very important in the stuff we do for the glory of God. Our role in all of this is serious because it affects others. If we decide to chill out in that thing we normally do for the Lord, the body of Christ is going to be affected. Because of that, we can't stop. We have to keep on keepin' on. We also have to encourage others to keep on moving, too.

We are all on the same team working together for the same purpose.

Love
1 Corinthians 13: 1-13

Love is the greatest gift of all and its available to everyone. It should be the spark that sets us in motion. Everything we do for the Lord should be done out of love – love for God and love for others.

In ministry or service, if we do the 'Jesus' stuff out of obligation or because we feel we have to, it won't be effective. People's lives will not be touched. If you think of your ministry as a 9-to-5 job, then the results will be the same as that of a regular job. You'll get tired and burned out. It won't bear spiritual fruit.

If I decided to feed the hungry because I didn't have anything better to do or because someone made me do it, then the only result will be that a hungry person got fed. But, if I did it because I loved that person, then my actions would show them love and will affect their life. Love breaks down walls that people build around themselves and it goes straight to their heart. It will create a positive change.

Verses 4 through 8 gives us examples of what love is:

Love is patient

Love is kind

Love doesn't envy

Love doesn't boast

Love isn't proud

Love isn't rude

Love isn't self-seeking

Love isn't easily angered

Love doesn't keep records of wrong

Love doesn't delight in evil

Love rejoices with the truth

Love always protects

Love always trusts

Love always hopes

Love always perseveres

Love never fails

The world can be cruel sometimes. There are things that happen in our lives that try to steal the gift of love away from us. Yes, we can love our families and a handful of selected friends, but what about loving everybody? That may be hard for us to do. It's especially hard to love someone that has done us wrong or whose life doesn't fit in with our scope of things. But, God wants us to love everybody — no matter who they are or what they've done. It could be those people who God intends for us to lead to Him.

Gifts of Prophecy and Tongues
1 Corinthians 14: 1-25

These verses bring up some topics that have been debated on for many years among the many divisions of churches out there. It's a touchy subject and people will argue about it. But, if you really want to know what God's Word is telling us, you'll have to study and read what is going on. You can't lock yourself on one line of scripture and use your imagination as to what it's talking about. You have to put it all together.

What are the gifts of prophesying and tongues? Most of what we know about them is from what people have told us. These folks will give reference to a line or two from the Bible and we will sorta take their word for it and leave the subject alone.

Since it's such a touchy subject, we won't question it out of fear of offending God. Even though we know we're saved and know that we don't have any of those gifts personally, it's easier to just leave it alone.

On the subject of speaking in tongues, I remember many years ago being in churches where some of it's members would stand up in the middle of a service and start speaking out loud in an unknown language. I will admit that it was weird and a little scary. I couldn't understand a word of it and assumed they were talking to God in their special language. I also thought that maybe these folks were special, as if they had a special connection with God that I didn't have. I thought maybe one day when my life became more holy, I would be given that gift. But, until then, I would just pray the best I could and hope that God would hear me.

After studying the Bible myself, I learned Jesus had a mission for

His disciples. Their job was to share the Gospel to the ends of the Earth. This mission applies to us, too. So, how do you share the Gospel, as an English-speaking person with someone from another country that doesn't have a clue to what you're saying? If the Lord puts you in that position, He will have to give you the tools to do it with. I am believing that speaking in tongues is the ability to speak to someone in their own language.

In the Book of Acts, the Holy Spirit gives the disciples the ability of speaking in tongues:

And when the day of Pentecost was fully come, they were all with one accord in one place. And suddenly there came a sound from heaven as of a rushing mighty wind, and it filled all the house where they were sitting. And there appeared unto them cloven tongues like as of fire, and it sat upon each of them. And they were all filled with the Holy Ghost, and began to speak with other tongues, as the Spirit gave them utterance.

And there were dwelling at Jerusalem Jews, devout men, out of every nation under heaven. Now when this was noised abroad, the multitude came together, and were confounded, because that every man heard them speak in his own language. And they were all amazed and marvelled, saying one to another, Behold, are not all these which speak Galilaeans? And how hear we every man in our own tongue, wherein we were born? Parthians, and Medes, and Elamites, and the dwellers in Mesopotamia, and in Judaea, and Cappadocia, in Pontus, and Asia, Phrygia, and Pamphylia, in Egypt, and in the parts of Libya about Cyrene, and strangers of Rome, Jews and proselytes, Cretes and Arabians, we do hear them speak in our tongues the wonderful works of God. - Acts 2:1-11

The key here is knowing that the Holy Spirit gave them the gift of speaking in tongues. This is the first time this happened and it's purpose was so that the foreigners could hear them in their own language. Are you getting the same thing?

Now as 'speaking tongues' is being mentioned throughout the Bible, would it's definition change? Would it go from being a tool to use when speaking to foreigners and then change to being a special prayer language between a person and God? I wouldn't think so.

One thing we learn from the Book of Corinthians is that the church in Corinth was having some issues. Paul was there to help them get their ducks in a row. In the verses from 14: 1-25, it seems the church was all excited about having spiritual gifts, especially the gift of speaking in tongues. If we assume the gift is speaking a foreign language, I imagine the church was noisy and nobody got anything out of the services. It was in disorder and probably very rowdy. But, the folks speaking it would look pretty cool.

Can you imagine going to your American church and hearing several people speaking in individual foreign languages? Whoa!! It would cause a head rush! The only one that could understand them would be God. Right?

In addition, why would God give only certain people a special prayer language that could only be used between Him and them? Since God loves the world, wouldn't He want everyone to talk to Him? For His own, I don't think He would make it so complicated.

Now how about prophesying? What makes it such an awesome gift to have? And while we're on the subject, what exactly is it?

Prophesying, to me, was one of those special gifts that God gave special folks. They were usually on the preaching TV stations, or had written several prediction books about the end times, and even the weird-acting people at church that were pretty smart on Bible knowledge. This gift gave them the ability to look deep into the future and see things that would one day happen. We knew folks like Nostradamus and the local palm reader wasn't of God because they didn't attend regular church services on Sunday. But, it was the ones that knew the Bible and could memorize scriptures. They stood out in the church crowd and looked the part. You know what I mean?

These verses tell us that prophesying edifies the church, which means it builds it up. It also says it convicts folks' hearts that they are sinners and brings their attention to God. And from other books of the Bible, prophesies were messages given to people by God to share with others and they weren't always about future events.

Aaron? Remember him? He was Moses' brother and was called a prophet. Moses was scared to speak to people, so God let Aaron do all the talking to Pharaoh.

And the LORD said unto Moses, See, I have made thee a god to Pharaoh: and Aaron thy brother shall be thy prophet. Thou shalt speak all that I command thee: and Aaron thy brother shall speak unto Pharaoh, that he send the children of Israel out of his land. - Exodus 7:1,2

Did Aaron walk around making predictions of future events? I don't think he did. He basically shared what God told Moses to tell him. Maybe that's what prophesying is all about — sharing God's message with people.

The Book of Revelation is considered a prophetic book. It tells the details of future events that lead to the end of the world. Is it because the God-inspired writer, John, is predicting the future? Or could it be that John is simply just sharing what God told him to write. Either way, would that make John a prophet?

There are 17 prophetic books in the Bible. The 4 major prophets are: Isaiah, Jeremiah, Ezekiel, and Daniel. Most of these books were written telling about future events. Are these men prophets because they predicted the future? Or could it be that they are prophets because they wrote what God wanted them to write?

And another thing, the Bible talks about false prophets. Are these people that walk around making bad predictions of things that don't come true? Or could it be the people that are sharing news of things that God didn't tell them to say or write?

I would say that prophesies are God-inspired messages that provide insight, warning, correction and encouragement to people. It will build up the church and glorify God. Prophets, then, would be the messengers.

Orderly Worship
1 Corinthians 14: 26-40

God is not a God of disorder but of peace. Can you imagine going to a God-filled church that had all of its ducks in a row and its stuff together? That would be pretty nice wouldn't it?

I guess the church in Corinth must have been a wild place to go to for services. The entire congregation may have had their own little special thing going on in the pews with everybody prophesying, tongue-speaking, revelating, or whatever else they were doing. I bet it was out of control and the folks walked out not getting anything from any of it. That would have been sad. Wouldn't it?

132

And what about the lost folks that came to church that day? With all that ruckus going on, how could they get what they needed, too? I imagine they walked out as lost as they were when they came in.

Paul was trying to help them out by providing them with some helpful guidelines for their church. He wanted them to limit the number of folks speaking at one time. That sounds simple enough.

This applies to us today. We, as a church, should keep order. I agree that we should share what God gives us with everybody and do it in an orderly fashion. And those prideful folks that like to be noticed probably should sit still and behave themselves. It's all about God and not about us. Everything we do should bring honor and praise to Him. You agree?

In addition to those problems Paul addressed, He even told the church to keep the women silent and that they shouldn't be allowed to speak at all. They should be submissive and if they had any questions in church, they should wait until they got home and then ask their husbands. He reminded them that it was disgraceful for women to speak in church anyway. Oooh... this could create some future problems with the church today.

I believe Paul wasn't saying that women shouldn't be part of the church team and take part in the services. He was talking directly to the church in Corinth who was getting a bad reputation of being a rowdy church. I think the women that were there were part of the problem. They may not have been as Biblically educated as their husbands, so instead of interrupting the services to ask questions, it was best to do it at home. That makes more sense.

There are too many scriptures in the Bible that shows how important women are when it comes to God's work. Sharing the Gospel is an endless job opportunity for anyone that is saved and should be done by all.

I believe these scriptures were addressing how a church should keep order. Folks will get more out it when we do.

The Resurrection of Christ

1 Corinthians 15: 1-11

A Christian means 'little Christ'. The foundation of Christianity is Jesus Christ. It's all because of Him that we are saved. We're cool with that, right?

Our belief as Christians is that Jesus died for our sins, he was buried, and then He rose on the third day. You with me so far?

So, why is His resurrection so important to us as believers? Ever thought on that before?

It tells us, as believers, that God, the One we serve, not only has the power to create the universe and everything in it, He also has the power to raise it from the dead. He has sovereign power over life and death. That's pretty cool!

Most religions out there don't believe in a resurrection. The same was true back in the day when Paul wrote this letter. The Greek culture back then didn't believe in all that 'raising folks from the dead' stuff. This teaching of a resurrection was new. They served man-made gods and practiced man-made religions that didn't promise a life after death.

But, not Christianity! Oh no! Hundreds of people witnessed Jesus' resurrection, and based on that fact, we know that there is

135

more out of life. The grave is just the beginning. The victory over death has been won folks!

The Resurrection of the Dead
1 Corinthians 15: 12-34

Here again the critical element of the Christian faith is that death is not the end. After we are dead and gone, our spirit will live on forever with God. Our example and proof of this is Jesus. His life, death, and resurrection that was witnessed by hundreds of people is what we hold on to.

By not believing it, what is the real purpose of living a Christian life? Yeah, it might make us better people while we are here on this Earth. And yeah, it might leave some good memories about us when we're gone. Don't get me wrong, because those are some cool things. But, being honest, living the Christian life comes with a lot headaches, heartaches, and we seem to suffer from a lot of junk. So, if we don't believe in the resurrection, what would be the point of going through all of this mess?

On the flipside, since the resurrection is a fact, our Christian life would make more sense. Everything we go through would be for a higher purpose that goes beyond the grave. Our work here on Earth would be to help lead others to Jesus and to benefit from His free gift of eternal life. It's all in what you choose to believe.

My hope is in Jesus! The closer I walk with Him, the more He reveals Himself to me. I know there is a greater place waiting for me when this one is gone. Don'tchu?

The Resurrection Body
1 Corinthians 15: 35-58

The Bible says we will be given new bodies. So, what are we going to look like? Will our friends and family recognize us? And how's it all going to happen anyway?

All we know is that it will happen fast like the twinkling of an eye. When the trumpet sounds, our dead bodies will rise and we will be changed. It will be a quick thing.

The verses give us a comparison of the bodies we have and what they will be in Eternity. We will go from having dishonored natural bodies that are weak and dying to glorified spiritual bodies that are powerful and eternal. That's good to know. Ain't it?

We are given a glimpse of what Jesus' body looked like after it was glorified:

"And was transfigured before them: and his face did shine as the sun, and his raiment was white as the light." - Matthew 17: 2

If we are being made into the image of Jesus, chances are we are going to have the same likeness, too. So, get ready for a bright wardrobe!

And will people know who we are? The Book of Matthew continues:

"And, behold, there appeared unto them Moses and Elias talking with him. Then answered Peter, and said unto Jesus, Lord, it is good for us to be here: if thou wilt, let us make here three tabernacles; one for thee, and one for Moses, and one for Elias." - Matthew 17: 3,4

My thinking is that if Peter recognized Moses and Elias, then chances are we will be able to recognize each other.

So basically, after we're all dead and gone, our spirits will live on in our new spiritual bodies that will last forever. We won't have to worry about sickness or diseases. We will be perfectly made into the image of Jesus. Our saved loved ones will be there and we will all know them.
Paul ends these verses with some direction. He tells us to 'stand firm and not to let anything move us'. We must dedicate ourselves fully to the work of the Lord. It won't be in vain.

The Collection for God's People
1 Corinthians 16: 1-4

Paul was basically getting the church at Corinth to take up donations that would help the Christian people in Jerusalem. These Christian folks were suffering from poverty and needed some financial help.

As Christians, we are to help those that need our help. It could be through a financial donation or we could help them by simply being there to listen and talk with them. We are encouraged to do this and it is mentioned a few times in the Bible.

Many of us have problems when it comes to giving others our money. I mean, it's ours because we worked hard for it. If we have extra money, we use it on whatever we want because it's ours. Right?

Wrong. Everything we have belongs to God. The job we have was because of a door opened to us by God. The paycheck we get is because God made it possible for us to get it. One thing I have learned is that God supplies everything. All that we have is because of Him. You agree?

If we understand and remember that fact, money becomes a tool that God gives us to do good works for Him. We have to be good stewards with it.

There are a lot of people in need in the world. Yes, each of us can't give to every charity that's out there. But, we can give to the ones that God sends our way. It could be to that person you meet at the gas station that is having a rough time financially. Or it could be a local charity group looking for people to give. The key here is to help when you can and when the Lord is telling you to.

Giving is a great witnessing tool. If people see us helping or is the ones we are giving to, it does something spiritually. Lives have changed because of the simple act of helping one another. We may not know the deeper problems of those people we help, but giving opens the door to their heart and they will see Jesus in us.

That's what giving is all about right there!

Personal Requests/Final Greetings
1 Corinthians 16: 5-24

Paul was a traveling man sharing the Gospel. He had many places to go. The problem with this is that it may have been hard for him to have relationships – a little one-on-one time with friends. Everything may have been in a rush.

I imagine people wanted to hang out with Paul for longer periods of time, but Paul had places to go and people to

meet. He was a man on a mission. But, he knew the importance of talking with people on a personal level.

For those of us in ministry, it's easy to do our thing and move on. The Lord is using us to do some mighty cool stuff for Him, but we can't forget the need for some one-on-one time. If people come into our life, we can't just push them off because we have more important things to do. We have to make time to share Jesus with them. Ya know?

Something that comes to mind is the role of a pastor. Yes, he has a big job in preaching to a congregation, but what about the person that sits in the pew that comes to him with a problem? Should he push them off to a deacon or a church counselor? Nope! He should schedule a time with them to talk about what's on their mind. Ministering to others has levels. We should do our best and be available to whoever God sends our way.

The cool thing is that Paul had people helping him in ministry. These verses mention Timothy, Apollos, Stephanas, Fortunatus, and Achaicus. There were also many others. Paul wasn't alone. In ministry, we may think that we are the only ones doing that cool thing that we do. But, it's not the case. God has people all over the world doing that same thing we do. Plus, the Lord will put people on your team to help you as well. We should never feel that we are carrying a full load. The Lord will provide you with everything you need to get the job done, whether it be the people or the material things. He's got us covered.

Paul ends this letter to the church in Corinth with a message of being on guard, standing firm in the faith and doing everything out of love for one another. This applies to us today. We should stay in God's Word, pray, and keep our spiritual stuff strengthened up. Satan is going to throw junk at us. We got to be ready.

If we're serving the Lord, we should do it out of love for Him and for other people out there. This is how we are going to lead them to Jesus. It's not the act of serving that does it. It's our motive behind why we serve. You see?

In summary, 1 Corinthians is about having unity and love in the church, because without it, it creates division. Jesus ain't all about that. One mind – one accord. We can't let the small petty stuff separate us. Satan loves to get church folks in an uproar. Just like a wolf in a sheep's pen, the first thing he does is separates them and then does a pile driver off the top rope on the weakest sheep. We should work more towards keeping the flock together and work out any differences. Most importantly as a group, stay focused on Jesus!

The Book Of
2nd Corinthians

The Book Of 2ⁿᵈ Corinthians

Introduction To 2ⁿᵈ Corinthians

Here again is another letter written by Paul to the church in Corinth around 55 – 57 A.D. Undoubtedly, the first book wasn't enough. Paul had a few more things to say.

The church at Corinth had some serious issues. Try to picture in your mind a church surrounded by an environment of idolatry and a bunch of immoral junk. This would affect anyone's faith and lifestyle – including Christians. It would be easy to get led astray and wander into something weird. That's exactly what was going on in Corinth. Paul was trying to help them, but was up against some obstacles. One of them being false teachers that were trying to add their two cents that taught the opposite of what Paul was teaching. It was a mess!

Paul writes 2 Corinthians and addresses those issues. We can apply it to our life and our walk with Jesus. Many of the things that went on back in the day are happening in the world today. Hopefully, we can all use it to make us stronger in the faith and possibly get rid of anything in our life that pulls us away from the Lord.

The God Of All Comfort

2 Corinthians 1: 1-11

God of all comfort?

Paul, as we already know, was a man chosen by God to deliver the Gospel all over the place. He was constantly moving. He had dedicated his life to doing what the Lord had called him to do. Paul was faithful and serious about it. You would think God would've made his journey a peaceful one. Right? Well, we know that wasn't the case.

Poor fella! Paul's journey was always up against some opposition. Some of those were life threatening. So, why did Paul have to go through so much junk when he was plainly doing what God had called him to do?

The word comfort in my mind means being able to live comfortably – no problems, no worries and no stress. I guess that's why money seems to be the only solution to our problems. If we come across a potential stressful situation, we can always solve it by throwing cash at it. Pretty simple.

And since God is a comfort provider, then He will always shower us with money to give us that free-flowing lifestyle that we rightfully deserve. Right?

Wrong. One thing I have learned from the Bible is that the Christian life is going to have struggles. Look at all of the people the Bible talks about and the stuff they have had to go through. Take a look at the life of Jesus. Wow! Can you imagine going through what He went through?

The day we decided to step out of our boat and follow Jesus was a life changing moment. We made a decision to allow God to change us and mold us to be more like Jesus. Becoming like Him doesn't happen overnight. It's a lifelong process that requires facing struggles. It's those problems we face that rebuilds our character and strengthens our faith. God comforts us by providing us with the strength, encouragement, and hope to deal with it. He works with us through it. This comforting relationship teaches us to love Him, instead of just coming to Him for a bandage or a quick aspirin. The comfort is knowing that He is always with us in all situations.

The extra cool thing is that we can share this comfort with others that may be going through something similar. By sharing what the Lord has done for us in that situation will be comforting to those that are just now going through it. You see what I'm saying?

Paul's struggles made Him stronger and more dependent on God to help him through it. It built his faith and he learned a bunch of stuff through his experience with God. This helped him to share the Gospel more effectively and to be an encouragement to others because he knew what he was talking about – because he lived it.

Paul's Change of Plans
2 Corinthians 1: 12 – 2: 4

Paul had intentions of revisiting the church at Corinth, but he had changed his mind. It wasn't because he was wishy-washy. He truly cared about them. It had more to do with the timing because the church still had unresolved problems. His visit could have made matters worse.

There are a few key points about Paul and his ministry that I received from these verses:

The way He conducted himself in

the world and around people – holy and sincere.

What does it mean to live a holy life? To me, it means to live according to God's Word in a way that's pleasing to Him. There are things mentioned in there that provide us with a better way of living. It shouldn't be looked at as a list of rules, but a way for us to get the most out of life.

The Bible tells us that Jesus came to give us life and give it to us abundantly. Living 'holy' isn't a bad thing. Some may see it as a boring way to live, but living this way offers peace and happiness. It's not stressful. If we could just understand God's love for us, then we would see that this relationship isn't a dictatorship. God's Word isn't a list of To Do's and Dont's, but more of a guideline to receive the good stuff that God freely offers us. Paul lived this life and wanted others to live it, too.

Paul was also sincere. He had a heart for people. Everything he did, he kept the feelings and thoughts of others in mind. He could've easily bopped folks over the head with the Good News and made everyone feel like crap for being sinners, but he didn't. Instead, he flashed a light on sin and provided people with an escape route on how to be forgiven. He knew his role as a traffic controller and showed them the way to Jesus. He did this because he cared for them.

This is how we should share Jesus with people. The Holy Spirit convicts their hearts and they will know that they are sinners and lost without Him. They don't need for someone to continuously gouge them with a branding iron in an attempt to score another point for the Lord. This ain't a game and we're not competing for points. This is a love mission to rescue the lost.

He made what he preached simple and easy to understand.

The Gospel is a simple message. Sometimes the world makes it too complicated. Many times it's because of pride. Sometimes people try to impress people with all of the spiritual stuff they know or they want people to recognize their status as a man or woman of God. Well, here's a pride buster. If you're saved today, you are also a man or woman of God. We are all on the same level – no one is special. We all have the same job to do. We don't have to over-complicate God's Word to make ourselves look good. We should be more about making our presentation as simple as possible so that everyone understands what we are sharing with them.

All walks of life need to hear this simple message. Just like Paul, what can we do to present it so that no one has questions about it?

He was anointed.

Anointed? I have heard that word before many times. It's usually from a religious crowd. I always got the impression that being anointed meant having a divine calling on your life that not many others had. If you were anointed, this would mean you were 'a chosen one' with special God-given abilities that could possibly help you leap tall buildings with a single bound. I have learned that ain't right.

If you're saved today, you're anointed, too. There are two things you receive when you choose to accept Jesus as your Lord and Savior:

1) **Seal of ownership**
2) **The Holy Spirit**

With these, you realize who your Master is – God. He gives us the Holy Spirit, who guarantees our salvation and the eternal life we will receive when Jesus returns. This is what being anointed is all about.

Forgiveness of the Sinner

2 Corinthians 2: 5-11

Sounds like the church in Corinth was having some issues with forgiveness. There may have been some folks that had some junk in their life and the church booted them out the door. They may of held a grudge against those people. Paul wanted the church to forgive them and comfort them.

I imagine the person or people being pushed away by the church felt like an outcast. Keep in mind, the purpose of church discipline is to restore fellowship and lead people to repentance of their junk. Making a person feel like an outsider only makes them bitter and eventually will make them hate 'going to church' all together.

Sin in a church will affect its ministry and purpose. I believe, if a person in some kind of leadership position has some junk going on in their life, they should be asked to step down until they get it squared up. As a church body, we shouldn't push them away like yesterday's trash. Instead, we should help them out of love to restore fellowship with the Lord and the church by working with them and helping them get their life together.

Satan can get a foothold in a situation like this by making the accusers feel all prideful about their holiness, while at the same time, making the accused feel like crap. With all them church fingers pointing at them, eventually they may begin feeling bitter toward Christian people, the church, and it may even push them further away from the Lord.

The message here is to maintain love for people through the good times and bad times in a person's life. Everyone is going to be tempted and attacked by Satan, including church members. Our job is to always be there for each other.

Ministers of the New Covenant
2 Corinthians 2: 12 – 3: 6

As Christians, we have a smell? But not just the outward odor that's created from excessive sweating, it's a spiritual one. To the folks that are dying in sin, we smell pretty good cause we are sharing Jesus' free gift of eternal life. This 'hope' smells all flowery and junk. We also wreak with the smell of death to some because we are shining a light on their sinful nature and we know this leads to death. That's pretty cool!

Paul wasn't the only one back in the day sharing the Word of God. Oh no! There were others. According to the scripture, some did it as a business and made money doing it. That doesn't mean that receiving an income from it was wrong, but maybe their only purpose for doing it was for the money. Paul took his job seriously, as a man sent from God, and he did it out of sincerity because he loved God and he loved people.

If you've ever stepped out to do ministry stuff, you will quickly realize that it's not a cash cow. Your step of faith doesn't earn you millions of dollars. If anything, you will probably go broke but you will find that your needs will be met. God may decide to bless your efforts and create a way for you to make an income from it, but don't let that be your focus. It's about having a passion for doing the Lord's work and doing what you can to lead folks to Him. It's about loving others and being sincere when you share Jesus with them.

If you're reading this book today, it's because God has chosen to use it and put it out there for folks to read. It's nothing I have done. I'm just a simple man, a small speck on this big planet. I'm currently unemployed with a laptop that has a screen that flickers. This is a step of faith for me because I am using my time to do something I feel the Lord has led me to do. I don't know what His plans are for it. But, I do know that I love people and if my talents lead someone to Jesus, then that would be pretty awesome!

Ministry work is a spiritual thing. You don't need special certifications to do it. You don't need a list of credentials. All you need to do is be willing to let God use you. Those gifts and talents you were born with, that God gave you, are the tools for you to use. The Holy Spirit that dwells within you will guide you and direct you in all that you do. It's about being available to God. We're not able to do this in our own strength and be effective. It's the power of God through us that gets the job done.

The Glory of the New Covenant
2 Corinthians 3: 7-18

Paul is talking to the church about the glory of the new covenant and comparing it to the old covenant. To better understand what he is saying, we would have to understand what all this covenant business is about.

Old Covenant
Back in the day of Moses, people lived their life trying to please God through sacrifices, offerings, vows, following a list of laws, and they had no direct access to God. There was a veil that

separated them. Only the Holy of Holies could go beyond this veil to communicate with Him.

Over time, this way of life became boring and dull. The people did their religious stuff out of duty and not out of a whole-hearted love for God. Sacrifices were made without a sincere regret for the sins they committed against Him. It was all just another routine that was almost impossible to follow.

New Covenant

For God so love the world that He sent His Son to die on the cross. This personal sacrifice was God's way of uniting the world to Him. By doing so, the veil that separated us was torn for those that turn to Jesus for Salvation. This sacrifice gave us, as Christians, freedom to communicate with God through Jesus.

On a spiritual sense, this veil represents sin. Our works and personal efforts cannot remove the veil (sin) that separates us from God. It is only through Jesus that our sins are forgiven and our veil removed. Does that make sense?

The glory part of all of this is that without the veil in our life, we can grow to be more like Jesus, with the Holy Spirit's guidance, and begin

glowing His likeness to the world around us.

I believe that is what Paul was sharing with the folks at Corinth from these verses. Some may have been trying to live life the old way.

Treasures in Jars of Clay
2 Corinthians 4:1-18

Satan is actively working in the world today and has caused a lot of folks to be blind. When someone shares the Gospel with them, they put up a block wall as if they didn't hear a word they said. These folks don't realize their sin separates them from God and that Jesus can free them from its chains and offer them eternal life.

Many of the preachers and teachers floating around out there share a message that pleases the audience. Its purpose is to draw crowds and make the people feel good, regardless of the sin in their life. If they are comfortable with being lost, they won't know what being saved is all about. This is a lie created by Satan.

Paul's message was a light in the darkness. He shared Jesus with folks. He didn't beef it up or try to impress them with anything fancy. He didn't try to draw attention to himself or make himself look good. He knew it wasn't about him, but about Jesus. He used the illustration of treasure in jars of clay to symbolize his role as a messenger of the Gospel. Jars of clay?

Clay, when made into jars, is fragile and its made from the Earth. It can be shaped into something that looks cool and useful, but it can easily be broken and cracked. Paul used this to illustrate how fragile we are as humans. We're not perfect. We go through some junk! Life can put a whoopin' on us and leave scars. But, as vessels sharing the Gospel, the treasure isn't the container. Its the message! It changes lives.

If we can realize how fragile we are, then we shouldn't be building up pride in our abilities, but focusing more on the message God is delivering through us. He is the power! We should make sure folks can see Him in us. Know what I mean?

And another thing I received from this is that we can't give up. We need to think more about the eternal life that we will have in the future. All of life's troubles and worries that we face today is a temporary thing. It will weigh us down if we let it, but we have to think outside of the box on what Jesus has in store for us when this life is over.

Our Heavenly Dwelling
2 Corinthians 5: 1-10

If you are saved today, you have a home built by God. It's not that single-wide trailer you have by the lake either. It's an eternal home made just for you by His hands. He gave His Holy Spirit to live within us as a deposit, a guarantee, of what is yet to come. Because of this, we don't have to be afraid of death. We have hope and confidence of an eternal life after this one is over with.

We can begin to look at life's problems in a different light. It's all just temporary; sickness, pain, sorrow, and worries will one day be gone. We have a brighter future because of Jesus and what He did for us on the cross. That's enough to get you excited right there.

As long as we walk this Earth, we are just traveling through. Our purpose here is to do the Lord's work and do everything we can to please Him while we are here. This includes living according to His Word, sharing Jesus with people, and living life to its fullest as children of God.

We have something to look forward to.

The Ministry of Reconciliation
2 Corinthians 5: 11 – 6: 2

I think what may be hard for some of us to fully understand is the fact that, without Jesus, we are separated from God. The sin in our life puts a brick wall up between us and our Creator. It could be that we don't realize how serious our sin is because we live in a world that waters it down.

When we compare the junk in our life against what we see and hear on TV, the radio, or out on the street, our sin may not appear to be so bad. We may think that we're cool in the eyes of God because we ain't as bad as some of those other folks out there. But, that's what Satan wants us to think. The sad thing is that the morality of the world is going to get worse and a lot of the junk today is going to be acceptable in the future.

Think about it. Look around you. How much of the things going on today was acceptable years ago? The big word here is 'desensitizing'. If Satan can get the world to overlook sin and make it acceptable, then it wouldn't be sin anymore in worldly eyes. If there is no sin, then what would be the purpose of being saved? What did Jesus die on the cross for?

Just so that you know, in God's eyes, it's still sin no matter what the world thinks. Sin separates us from God. But because of Jesus, He made an attempt to draw folks to Himself. This is the message Paul was preaching and should be the one we are sharing with the world.

You see, by asking for forgiveness of our sins and accepting Jesus as our Lord and Savior, we are trading our sin for His righteousness. We are forgiven for the junk in our lives. We are then reconciled with God.

That's what it's all about.

Paul's Hardships
2 Corinthians 6: 3-13

If you look back on Paul's life to this point, you would see a change. This dude was living a comfortable life in the military as a Christian killer and probably made a good living at it. It probably had some awesome fringe benefits with a great 401K plan. Maybe a few weeks vacation and a company chariot. Who knows?

Then he met Jesus on Damascus Road and his life was transformed. That's good news, right? But what about those cool fringe benefits? He lost them in pursuit of a calling in his life to share Jesus with the same folks he wanted to kill. He may have went from a comfortable life to a life full of headaches and troubles. Was the change worth it?

You would think, as a messenger of God, Paul would have been given the holy path on Easy Street. But, from the sounds of it, it appears that Paul went through some junk for the sake of sharing the Gospel. Some of us would have given up or became angry and bitter at God for allowing this to happen. I mean, we're doing Him a favor by delivering His mail. The least He could do is provide us with a cozy mail delivery vehicle to do it with. Right?

One of the lessons I am learning in ministry is the battle we have with ourselves. We are prideful people whether we know it or not. We look out for number one – and that's us. Even though we may be doing God's work, those conflicts in our life become a test for us to see how sincere we are about doing God's work. It becomes a battle.

As long as sharing the Gospel meant comfort, it wouldn't be that big of a deal for doing it. But when you become a target for some bad junk, it's not so cozy. You are left with a choice. You can stop doing it and get back on Easy Street or you can realize that you're doing it for the Lord and stay on the Hard Road.

Suppose God called you to preach and you learned that it's illegal to preach or you're called to do it where folks will kill you for doing it. Do you continue preaching and take the consequences or stop because you're looking out for your best interest? Your choice determines who you're doing it for.

It's a test of the heart. But know that if we discover the true sincerity and humbleness of our heart is for the Lord, He will be able to use us for some mighty works for Him. People are going to be led to Him through you. Folks are going to be saved.

Wouldn't that be cool?

Paul knew that God was in charge of His life and directed his path. In all of the bad situations, Paul knew that God put him there and could use him. The times Paul was placed in jail, God used him to preach to the prisoners and guards. In the times of persecution, Paul stayed true to God and people were encouraged through his actions.

God has a purpose behind everything we go through. We shouldn't focus on ourselves so much and stay true to God. We should trust Him to know that He is God and knows what He is doing through our lives.

Do Not Be Yoked With Unbelievers
2 Corinthians 6: 14 – 7: 1

From the sounds of these scriptures it's almost like it's saying stay away from sinners. I mean, we're Christians and we're all pure and junk. We don't want any of that 'sinner stank' getting on us. So maybe we should all like separate ourselves from them and huddle up as Christian brothers and sisters and build a wall that keeps the poo out. Know what I'm saying?

That just doesn't sound like the right thing to do. Jesus didn't act like that. He was all over the place hanging out with sinners, but yet remained sinless. So what exactly are these scriptures trying to say?

Yoke? What is a yoke? I always thought it was how the toothless people said the word 'joke'. But, I guess it's a real word. The dictionary tells us that a yoke is a wooden bar that connects the heads and necks of animals together. The purpose is to join them so that they can work together. A yoke is a farming tool to help with plowing a garden and junk. It's also used in maintaining the horsepower of your covered wagon by making the old school pistons (animals with legs) work together. Unfortunately, I don't think we use yokes anymore. But, the key here is that it helps animals work together.

Since the subject is about working together, Paul is telling the church at Corinth to not form binding relationships – personal or business – with folks that weren't Christian believers. It would cause conflict in the relationship.

An example would be forming a business partnership. One of the owners would be all about God, while the other wasn't. One would conduct their side of the business according to God's Word, while the other would possibly follow money and do whatever it takes to bring it in – whether it's morally acceptable or not. The Christian fella could compromise his faith and loyalty to God by handling business the way his partner does.

Another example is about marriage. Let's say a Christian woman decides to marry a man that was an unbeliever. What could possibly go wrong in this situation? Well, since marriage is a spiritual bond, it would be like mixing water with oil – it don't mix. The simple thing of worshiping God, the woman is going to be up against some opposition from her spouse. She may compromise her faith in order to make her husband happy. This unequally yoked relationship will affect the kids. Which way will they go?

Yoking with unbelievers isn't about hanging out with folks that don't know Jesus as Lord and Savior. Actually we should be a light in their darkness by spending a little time with them and sharing Jesus with them. The problem happens when we join forces and work together as a unit. There will be some conflict that may cause us to compromise our faith.

I believe that is what Paul was saying.

Paul's Joy
2 Corinthians 7: 2-16

Paul had joy, despite all of the problems he had faced in ministry — harassment, conflicts, and fear. How could he have joy while going through so much junk? I believe the answer is that he saw the folks at Corinth changing.

165

They began realizing where they stood in sin and asked for forgiveness from God. They took the right steps towards a change in the way they lived. It was through Paul's ministry that helped them realize their wrong.

Yeah, he might of wrote them a letter explaining some of the wrong stuff they were doing. And yeah, it might of hurt their feelings for a little while. But Paul did it out of love and because of that, these folks began changing. The way to lead people to Jesus is to first love them. When we love them first, we can then point their sins in the direction of the cross.

These verses talk about sorrow and mentions two types: Godly sorrow and worldly sorrow. We can be sorry for the sin in our life, but the difference is in why we are sorry. Having Godly sorrow is when we realize that our actions go against God. Worldly sorrow is when we are sorry for our actions only when we get caught. Godly sorrow leads to repentance and changes lives.

A thought comes to mind is ministries that visit jails and prisons. They preach Jesus to the prisoners and many of them get saved. But it seems as soon they get released back to the real world, they begin acting like they did before they got in there. Were they sincere with their

166

prayer for salvation and sorry for their sin with Godly sorrow? Or was it just a worldly sorrow? Their new life will reflect it.

Generosity Encouraged
2 Corinthians 8: 1-15

Paul encouraged the church in Corinth to give. He was writing this letter while in Macedonia and used them as an example of giving. Even though they were poor, they gave more than he expected. This is called sacrificial giving. The point here is not in the amount they gave, but the 'heart' in which they gave.

You see, this church in Macedonia gave to the Lord. They had love for the Lord's work and the ministers He had called for His purpose. This should be the example of how we should give – give freely.

I know there are a lot of churches and cool Christian TV preachers out there that urge folks to give. Some preach a prosperity message that tells you that God will give you financial blessings based on how much you give them. If you give them a dollar, you will find ten dollars mysteriously in your checking account. This type of preaching makes it sound like giving to a church is similar to playing the stock market or investing in the 401K plan. That's not how it works. Yes, God loves a cheerful giver and does bless those that give. He even provides His faithful people with a means to give. I believe that. But, the reason we give shouldn't be so that we can receive a good return on our investment. It should be because we love the Lord and want to be good stewards with what He has given us. This also means not taking away from our family's needs in order to give either.

If we have plenty, it's probably because God wants us to share it with someone in need. As Christians, we should want to be part of organizations that help people. That's what Christians do because that is what Jesus did. He's our example.

Titus Sent To Corinth
2 Corinthians 8: 16 – 9: 5

Titus was carrying a financial gift to Jerusalem, but he wasn't by himself. A 'brother' was coming along with him. I would assume the reason was because people were judgmental when it came to someone handling money for the church. All eyes were on them. This 'brother' was like an eyewitness that Titus wasn't doing anything shady. Ya know?

Maybe they were worried that Titus would make a few pit stops and use their funds on personal stuff. He may of wanted to play a few rounds of putt putt golf at the Desert Sand Entertainment

Park along the way. Or maybe he would blow the money on a brand new pair of designer brand running sandals. Having a 'brother' along for the ride would help keep the peace.

This can be applied to us today. For churches out there, it would be wise to set up a team of folks to handle the church money. This will prevent people from making accusations against it.

Write everything down and keep good accounting records. We're handling the Lord's money and we should be wise with it. It just makes good sense.

Titus? All we know about Titus was that he was a disciple and companion of Paul and that he did some cool ministry work. He even has a book in the Bible named after him that has three neat chapters. Paul had respect for him to consider him a partner. That's pretty cool!

Sowing Generously
2 Corinthians 9: 6 – 10: 18

God loves a cheerful giver. You've heard that before, haven't you? It may have been from one of them money-grabbin' TV evangelist or it could have been from an honest God-called preacher in a sermon that's speaking the truth. God does love a cheerful giver and He wants us to give. But our hearts have to be right when we do.

I think the problem we have in giving is that we question the motives behind the person or group that is wanting our money. Even though our hearts may tell us to give, we question them:

"What are they going to spend my hard earned money on?"

"Why do they want me to give to them?"

My church had a gathering one time at a park where a bunch of folks got to together. We grilled out some food and sorta just hung out with each other. A guy walked up to a group of us and asked if we had any money to spare to give him. He told us how he was down on his luck, times were tough, and he needed some money to get him through. His words touched the hearts of a couple of us and we gave him some money. No big deal!

The next thing I know, a guy from our church comes up to us and says, "Dude, why did ya'll give him some money? All he's gonna do is buy some beer with it. He's an alcoholic."

We didn't know that he was an alcoholic and didn't think to question what he would be buying. Our hearts told us to give. This event has stayed with me and has left me wondering, "When is the right time to give?"

I believe we did the right thing that day in giving to the man regardless of his intentions. Our hearts were right. God has the power to provide, so regardless of what we did, God is in charge anyway. We showed our Christian character by giving and doing what the Lord expects from us. If we were tricked, then that's between them and God. And He will continue supplying my needs according to His Word. I win either way.

In Chapter 10, it seems that Paul was telling them how shy he was when it came to confrontations. When he didn't have to face people, he was bold. This let's me know that he was a simple man with a life-changing message. But, people were always questioning him. I guess they wanted to hear this message from someone with more outward elegance. They may have thought his letters were bold, but in person, Paul was nothing more than a mere wet chihuahua nipping at their ankles. They weren't impressed.

Paul knew the power that was behind what he was preaching. He had seen it change lives. This power came from the Lord. That's why He was so obedient in doing what the Lord wanted him to do.

The message to me from this would be, that if God has called you to do something, just do it. Don't focus on your weaknesses. Don't focus on the opposition that comes your way. God is working through you and you are just the vessel He has chosen to use. Keep your eyes on the power source.

Paul and the False Apostles

2 Corinthians 11: 1-15

Paul had a fear that the church in Corinth would fall victim of some of the false preachers and teachers out there. He wanted them to stay true to Jesus with sincere devotion and to hold firmly to the Gospel that they first accepted. Why?

Just like in today's world, there's a lot of weird junk being preached that's not of Jesus. It may appear to be the 'gospel', but it's not. Satan is using folks out there to share false doctrine and appearing to be an angel of light. People are gladly taking it all in and being deceived.

The way we can protect ourselves is to compare what these preachers and teachers tell us with what the Bible says. Follow along with them by reading the scriptures they quote from. Take your Bibles to church. Don't be so mesmerized by how cool these preachers look; their certifications and degrees,

172

their million dollar wardrobe, expensive cars, homes, and their smooth speaking techniques they learned in college. Focus on what they're saying — the content. Does it match the Bible? If not, you may want to move on.

On another note, to lose devotion for Jesus would involve filling that time with other time consuming things. If Satan can't make you sin against God, he can keep you busy to where you're not focused on Him. By not having the Lord as a number one priority in your life, you will become spiritually weak and could fall victim to temptations and the junk that Satan throws at you.

The church at Corinth must have had their mind on their money and their money on their mind. That may have been why Paul was cautious about asking them for anything. It may have diluted what they heard from his message. He knew that he was being judged so he may have felt that by charging them a fee would add fuel to the fire.

I also get the impression that the church may have ranked their guest speakers by how much they charged them. The good speakers would be the ones that charged a lot and the poor speakers would be the ones knocking on their doors to do it for free. As a church today, we have to be more focused on the content that is being said and compare it with what the scriptures tell us.

Paul Boasts About His Sufferings
2 Corinthians 11: 16-33

In these verses, Paul is speaking from the heart. He was letting it all out. You would think he was bragging about all of the cool things he had went through in ministry. To make himself look all cool and junk, you would think he was trying to make folks think he was the Chuck Norris of Gospel-sharing. That wasn't the case.

The church in Corinth were getting misled by all of

these false teachers. They liked the idea of how well they spoke with authority, they dressed with elegance, and possibly how cool their tour bus looked parked in front of their church. I believe Paul was making a point of how none of them suffered for Christ's sake like he did. As we have learned, Paul had sacrificed his life for the Gospel.

As Christians stepping up to the plate to serve the Lord in ministry, we are going to go through some challenges. We are going to be beat up spiritually, made fun of, and body slammed with discouragement. But, this is part of the character-building process. There's something about going through it that builds our faith and prepares us for serving the Lord.

The next time you see someone that claims to be a servant of God, look for the battle scars.

Paul's Vision and His Thorn
2 Corinthians 12: 1-10

OK. These verses got a little weird for me. It talks about visions, revelations, third heavens, and out of body experiences. What's this all about?

Paul starts theses verses by saying he's gonna keep on boasting, even though there is nothing to gain from it. He is still trying to convince the church of his credentials as a man of God. He goes on to talk about visions and revelations that were given to him from the Lord.

I believe a 'vision' in this case would be a spiritual experience that could only be seen with spiritual eyes. And the 'revelation' would be information he received that only he witnessed of something that he hadn't already known. Are you following me?

I think Paul saw and heard something that changed his life. The Lord may have provided him with some spiritual insight that would strengthen him in doing His work. Paul may have kept this a secret until now because people may have thought he was nuts. Or they would've focused more on these spiritual 'novelties' instead of the messages Paul was giving.

Paul continues talking about a man, a Christian fella, that 14 years ago was caught up into the third heaven. He also calls it 'paradise' where this man heard stuff that can't be expressed; things that man can't tell. Ooh! Sounds kinda mysterious, doesn't it?

Who was this man Paul was talking about? Could it have been himself that he was speaking of? Did Paul have an out of body (or in-body) experience that took him to heaven where God is? It's possible.

And what about that thorn in his side? Did Paul fall into a rose bush? Or was it a sickness that God wouldn't heal him of? Verse 7 says this thorn was a messenger from Satan (a demon?) to torment him and to keep him from being conceited because of the revelations he had received. That's interesting.

What we do know is that Paul depended on God for strength in his ministry. He couldn't rely on himself. The same is true for us. We can't save people! Only by God's power working in us can people's lives change. That's the deal!

Paul's Concern For The Corinthians
2 Corinthians 12: 11-21

Sounds like Paul was worried about them. He was wanting to visit them for the third time. I think he was also concerned that they wouldn't accept him and may have thought of him as a burden to their church.

It seems that all through his letter to Corinth he mentioned that he didn't want to ask them for any financial help. Even though he had received it from other churches, it's like he refused to take a hand out from them. He was more concerned with preaching to them with the hopes that they would change their ways and stay true to Jesus. He was on fire about that.

This church must have been very judgmental of him because it seems he was always trying to justify himself to them. It's like they put him 'on trial' and he had to plead his case. It wasn't so that he could maintain his good reputation, but he was concerned of what people would think of Jesus. He wanted them to know Him like he knew Him.

From verse 21, it seems Paul was afraid that on his third return to Corinth, he would find them in a mess because they were allowing junk in the church.

He mentions a list of sins that they may fall victim to and how sad he would be about it. He worked hard for this church that he founded. The things he did for them was for their benefit. I imagine it would be hard to see this church crumble after you warned it several times.

As a church today, we have to be very careful. We can't allow this immoral world to change us. We have to hold true to our values that we have learned from the Bible.

If we, as a church, become desensitized as the world has, we are going to be in bad shape, too. Just like the church at Corinth.

Final Warnings & Greetings
2 Corinthians 13: 1-14

Paul ends his letter with some

warnings to the church – this would be his third and final warning. I imagine when he got there, he would be throwing some folks out the door and revoking some church memberships. Not good!

Paul speaks of a way for them to test their faith by truly examining themselves. This applies to us. By looking at our life spiritually, we should

179

know if we are about Jesus or not. It should show in how we act and treat others. We should be seeing fruit and should be growing as Christians. If not, then we are not where we are supposed to be. We need to square that up and get back on track.

When was the last time you read the Bible or prayed? Have you been to church lately? Are you closer to Jesus than you were last week? It's these spiritual check-ups that lets us know where we stand. It's sorta like getting a physical at the doctor's office. We should do it often. Believe it or not, our goal is perfection just like Jesus.

The Book Of
Galatians

The Book Of Galatians

Introduction To Galatians

The book of Galatians could be summarized as a book about freedom. As Christians, our salvation is not bound to a list of laws that we have to follow. It's by faith in Jesus. We are not bound to our old sinful nature because Jesus set us free. We are saved because we stepped out on faith to accept God's free gift of salvation and it's by His grace that He offered it to us to begin with. We're free! That's pretty cool stuff! Ain't it?

Paul wrote this letter back around A.D. 49 to the churches in Galatia that he helped start. I'm not really sure where that is, but I can almost guarantee you that it wasn't in the United States. It seems the Jewish folks were telling the Gentiles that in order for them to truly be saved was to start following this big ol' list of Jewish rules and junk. But, Paul knew better and whipped his feathery pen out and wrote them about it. He wanted to set the record straight.

There's gonna be some good stuff coming from this letter that Paul wrote that we can apply to our lives as Christians. I'm sure we can all learn a thing or two from it. It never hurts to dig in to God's Word and gain some Biblical knowledge and some spiritual nourishment. I hope you're hungry.

So, grab your Bibles. If you have to go to your car and get it off the dashboard, I'll wait. I ain't going anywhere.

The key is to get what God has in store for us from reading Galatians. It's a small book, so we can take it slow if we want to.

No Other Gospel
Galatians 1: 1-10

Paul begins his letter by explaining to them straight up that he was sent by God and not by men. I guess he felt this was how he should start his letter to the church in Galatia — by addressing his authority and where it came from. By doing this, it would let them know that he would be speaking from the heart with his God-inspired message. And they could be confident to know that he wasn't doing it for any selfish

reasons. They would know that he was a man on a mission. For Paul, knowing that he was sent by God, he could speak (or write) with boldness because God would be working through him. That's power right there!

We can have that confidence, too. As Christians on a God-called mission, we can walk boldly holding our head high and speak in the authority given to us by God. On the flip side, if you're doing stuff on your own and in your own strength, you might as well sit down. It won't pack a punch. It would be like lighting matches under water.

The church in Galatia was founded by Paul and was preached the Gospel... the true Gospel. So in the beginning, they had their junk together. But, over time it seemed as if they were drifting away from what they were originally taught and sorta floated over to some weird gospel that was being preached to them. The church was now confused. How in the world did that happen?

I believe it begins with laziness and a lack of confidence. God has supplied us with everything we need to know in His Word, but yet many of us don't take the time to read it. Instead we rely on preachers to read it to us and explain it. In many cases, we don't even open up our Bibles and follow along with them. We simply take their word for it and believe that, just because they're preachers, everything they say is the truth. This opens the door to receive false information.

It could also be that we try and read the Bible, but instead of relying on the Holy Spirit to teach us, we get spiritual A.D.D. and get all confused. We develop a lack of confidence and get discouraged. We put the Bible down. Here again, we rely on someone else to teach us what they think the Bible says.

Just because a smooth-talking person preaches it, it doesn't make it right. Read for ourselves and allow the Holy Spirit to give us the details.

Paul Called By God
Galatians 1: 11-24

We all remember the story of how Paul started his journey as a man of God on a mission to share the Gospel with the world. Right?

The fella was a Jew and his job was to persecute Christians. I'm not talking about simply 'making fun of them'. Paul had them killed. It was serious!

Then on Damascus road, as he was doing his regularly scheduled Christian killing, he was bopped with a light from the sky. From this point his life was changed. He began preaching the faith that he once tried to destroy. That's pretty cool!

But, here in these verses, Paul is trying to explain to the church in Galatia of his credentials. He wasn't taught by man, he didn't hold a worldly degree with a certificate on his wall or a flashy neon church sign hanging off the side of his camel. He was just a man that God chose to share the Gospel – and God was his strength and seal of approval. That's all he needed.

Many times we focus too much on why we are not qualified to do anything for the Lord. We may think we talk funny, look weird, or we're uneducated on Bible stuff. We may see all of our weaknesses and feel like God couldn't use us. So, instead, we just sit. But, He can. It's not our abilities that makes us usable. It's our total surrender to Him that He is able - cause He's the One that will be working through us anyhow. Right?

But, this doesn't mean we shouldn't spend time with God in prayer and studying His Word. It's like running a race. You have to put effort in it.

Paul Accepted by the Apostles
Galatians 2: 1-10

Instead of Paul busting the church doors open and rudely preaching to the masses, he showed courtesy and shared his message with the church leaders first. I imagine an average person would get a lot of 'stares' and 'judgment' if he started preaching in front of people. They would want to know, "Who is this guy?" or "Who does this guy think he is?"

I assume Paul had to get approval from the leaders so that it would make it more easier for the congregation to accept him. He was now 'pre-approved' like we are on those credit card advertisements we get in the mail.

Preaching the Word and sharing the Gospel comes with some opposition. You would think it would mostly come from folks that have never heard it before. But, the reality is that the biggest obstacle comes from other Christians. They will put the magnifying glass on you, study your life, and do a background check. But, if their pastor puts his stamp of approval on what you're doing, then they probably won't even question it. In ministry, it's probably best to share your vision first with the leaders of the church and people with authority that people respect. Not that we need their approval to do what we do, but it will help advance what we're doing for the Lord.

It seems that some 'false brothers' wormed their way into the group and began putting some of their 'religion stink' on them. Ya know the 'you gotta do this' or 'you gotta do that' in order to be all 'good' in God's eyes type of thing. But, Paul saw it coming and was ready for it. They didn't fall in their trap. And he wasn't impressed or moved by the 'know it alls' or the ones that thought they were 'all that and a bag of chips'. He stood his ground as a messenger of God – an apostle to the Gentiles.

It never fails. Someone always has some 'religious' advice to offer to help us in our ministry efforts. Some of it might be helpful, but I can guarantee you that if doesn't match what the Bible says or if it's 'manmade mumb-jumbo', it won't help share the simple message of the Gospel. If anything, it will over-complicate things and freak people out that need the Lord and push them away. We gotta KISS it (Keep It Simple, Stupid). Know what I'm sayin'?

The apostles – James, Peter, and John – accepted him. Paul thought that was cool and I'm sure they all did their high-fives and manly fist punches. They all agreed on one thing – to remember the poor.

Remembering the poor must have been an important issue. There may have been a bunch of po' folks living in the area. But, throughout the Bible there are many scriptures that talk about how believers should help the widows and the poor. I believe this applies to the world today.

As Christians, we should do what we can to help people. Give them food, money, clothing, or whatever they need to make it another day. I know our lives are busy and we should take care of our own family. But, when we reach a point of having an over-abundance in our own home, we should stop and think about those less fortunate. Instead of judging them for their condition, we should do something to help them get out of it. Plus, it's

Biblical.

Paul Opposes Peter
Galatians 2: 11-21

Whoa! That's something you wouldn't expect coming from the Bible. Two 'good fellas' opposing each other. In one corner, you got Paul, a converted Christian slayer weighing in at however much he weighed. In the other corner, you have Peter, a fisherman who was part of the original 12 that chose to follow Jesus. Peter was packing some experience under his championship belt and actually saw Jesus face to face. And now Peter and Paul had boxing gloves on? Say what??!!

Here's the deal. Peter and Paul, not to be confused with the 70's rock group, were Jews. Peter had the responsibility of sharing the Good News with the Jews. Paul shared it with the Gentiles. Sounds good so far?

The message of Salvation is that it's a free gift that anyone can receive from Jesus; God's Son that died on the cross for our sins and rose again on the third day. Salvation isn't something that you work towards. You don't have to follow a list of laws to get it.

Jesus already paid the price for it. It's there for the askin'. It's a faith thing. You still with me?

It seems that our buddy Peter was adding a little Jewish tradition into the mix. He was expecting new converts to start following Jewish laws. He also refused to hang out with Gentiles in fear of what the other Jews would say. Paul was saying, "Dude! That's just wrong!"

As Christians, we have freedom. Our salvation is secured. It's not 'what we do' or 'what we don't do' that determines if we're saved. Jesus took care of all that on the cross. It's having faith in Him – asking for forgiveness of our sins and asking Him to step into our life and take over.

Based on scripture, we have a freedom to do what we please after that... BUT... Jesus wants us to live righteous lives and follow Him. Not as a dictator, but out of love for us cause He wants us to live productively and be happy. He doesn't promote sin. Sin separates us from God, but it doesn't make us lose our salvation. That's going to offend some religious groups right there.

Faith or Observance Of The Law

Galatians 3: 1-14

Abraham, a familiar name from the Old Testament, was a 'righteous' dude. It wasn't because he was so cool with his sunglasses and designer clothes. God considered him righteous because of his faith. Abraham did stuff that God wanted him to in spite of his own personal feelings about it. He stepped out of his comfort zone and into the unknown where Jesus is (like the Casting Crowns' song says).

So, what did Abraham do that God liked so much? It was how he lived his life – on faith. God told him to sacrifice his son at an altar. Abraham was willing to do it. Abraham prayed for God to bless him with kids. Despite his old age, he kept believing and God answered. God built a nation under him.

It's this 'faith thing' that God likes. In our life, we have many opportunities to put our faith to the test. I believe God puts those opportunities there to see how we will react.

Our salvation is freely given and asks us to believe. Out of faith, we believe that Jesus died on the cross for us, rose again, and that by sincerely praying to Him for forgiveness of our sins and asking Him to come into our life, we will be saved. That's faith!

And it's simple!

Many of the church folk in the 'old days' may have questioned this simple plan for salvation. That's what it sounds like to me in these verses. They may have thought they had to do something to 'earn it', like following a bunch of laws.

The big word in all of this is called 'justified'. It's how we are made 'right' in God's eyes. It's not done by following the Golden Rules. Our sinful nature makes this process hard and we will work ourselves to death trying to do it and never achieve our goal. But, by accepting Jesus' free gift of salvation, we are justified before God. The Holy Spirit will dwell within us and give us the power we need to live for Him.

If you are working your way to Eternity by doing 'good', you might as well stop. Get your life squared up by accepting Jesus in to your heart. And because of this new change, the Holy Spirit will help you do 'good'. This takes faith!

The Law And The Promise
Galatians 3: 15-25

A couple of cool words that stand out to me from these verses is 'law' and 'promise'. You see, God gave Moses these laws and expected him and his people to live by it. These laws contained God's standards for living and revealed His very nature. Because of these laws, folks realized that they were sinful and that these laws were hard to follow.

Hundreds of years later, God made a promise to Abraham to build a nation that was pleasing to Him. This required faith on Abraham's part to trust God to see it come to pass because Abraham was old and childless. But, God delivered, and through Abraham's bloodline, Jesus was born.

And because of Jesus, all of us that are 'saved', we are part of that 'promise' that God gave and we are in that 'nation' that God built.

To sum it up, the law of the Old Testament revealed the world's sinful nature. This led to this faith that we have in Jesus, the Deliverer of God's promise. Did that make sense?

Sons Of God

Galatians 3: 26-4: 7

These are powerful verses right here. If you are saved today, you are a child of Almighty God. It doesn't matter what color your skin is or what country you live in. It doesn't matter if you're a man or a woman. We're all the same! If we belong to Jesus, we are seeds of Abraham. Dude, that's awesome stuff to know right there! Ain't it?

This tidbit of spiritual knowledge breaks barriers of racial tension, language, and gender. This tells me we are all on the same spiritual playing field. None of us is better than the other! We are brothers and sisters in Christ!

What would this mean in the world today? For starters, as a child of God, the color of your skin doesn't make you any better than anyone else. Just because you're a man or a woman, it doesn't make you superior to the other. Your income level in this world doesn't mean 'a hill of beans' in the kingdom of God.

Knowing this fact, we should hold our heads up high and love each other as brothers and sisters should. We're family!

Paul's Concern For The Galatians

Galatians 4: 8-20

It seems the Galatians had lost their joy of being saved. They were falling back on the ritualistic side of religion. This would involve celebrating special religious days and doing the whole ceremonial-type junk. This is called 'legalism' because you're following some religious 'legal' process of worship. That ain't cool!

There's freedom in being a Christian. God loves us and we should love Him and others. That's pretty much it in a nutshell. When we start following church rules, church people and their traditions, we miss out on the relationship that God wants to have with us.

Legalism turns God's love for us into something we try to earn and that's not how it should be. God's love is free! It makes being a Christian something no one would want because folks would think it's about trying to follow a list of rules that's hard to follow. The Good News would then come across as the 'bad news'. You see?

196

You want joy in your salvation? Begin making steps to a relationship with God by talking to Him in prayer. Study His Word and allow Him to speak to you. Go to church because you want to know more about your Father in Heaven, not because of your job duty that you have in the church.

And quit trying to live your Christian life trying to please others. Live your life for Jesus!

Hagar And Sarah
Galatians 4: 21-31

We learn from the Bible that Abraham had two sons. He prayed to have kids, and while he and his wife, Sarah, was waiting for God to answer, he took it upon himself to make it happen. He had a one night stand with a woman named Hagar.

Hagar was a servant (a

slave) and was the mother of Abraham's son, Ishmael. Her life symbolizes those who think we have 'to make it happen' by doing works to get favor from God. Sarah, who wasn't a slave or servant to no one (she was free), gave birth to Isaac, Abraham's son. He was a 'promise' that God gave to them and it required their faith in Him to see it through. Sarah's life represents how faith in Jesus delivers the free gift of Salvation that God promises everyone that believes.

This is what Paul is trying to explain to the people in Galatia. Here again, it's faith not works. It's not what we do in our own strength that saves us. It's faith in Jesus!

Freedom In Christ
Galatians 5:1-15

The fact that faith in Jesus is what saves us, there's freedom in that. This means we don't have to follow a bunch of laws and regulations to be saved. However, Paul warns the folks in Galatia, to not let this freedom give them the right to 'soak in the sin'. This applies to us.

Just because we're saved and promised eternal life with God, we shouldn't use this freedom to indulge in sinful junk. God

commands us to love one another. We shouldn't allow this freedom to make others stumble. Our life should reflect the One that saved us and lead them to Him. If we love them, we would want them to be saved, too. Knowing that sin separates us from a relationship with God, our sinful actions will push people away from Him as well.

Let's say a Christian exercises his freedom and decides to do a sinful act in front of folks. Those people he has confessed his Christianity to or witnessed to are going to say, "If this is what being a Christian is all about, I don't want no part of it." That's why it's important to live a life that leads folks to Jesus. We should use Jesus' example here on Earth, that we read about in the Bible, as a life to become.

The key to this life is found by loving one another.

Life by the Spirit
Galatians 5:16-26

As Christians, there's always a spiritual battle going on. Because we're human, we have a sinful nature. We're just born with it. It's there! I have one. You have one. You know that sweet old lady at Wally World that greets you at the door? She has one, too.

Our sinful nature goes against God's plans for us. If

we choose to follow this nature, we can be guaranteed that we'll be going against what God expects. The answer is to live by the Spirit. This is the Holy Spirit that dwells within us that's been there from the day we got saved. We should follow His leading.

These verses compares the differences in the two:

Sinful nature
- sexual immorality
- impurity
- debauchery
- idolatry
- witchcraft
- hatred
- discord
- jealousy
- fits of rage
- selfish ambition
- dissensions
- factions
- envy
- drunkeness
- orgies

Fruits of the Spirit
- love
- joy
- peace
- patience
- kindness
- goodness
- faithfulness
- gentleness

- self-control

To have an awesome Christian life would be to live by the Spirit. It's not a lifestyle that happens over night, but it's one that we can grow into as long as we stay on the path following Jesus. This would involve studying God's Word, praying, and striving to do as He says.

Doing Good to All
Galatians 6: 1-10

What should we be doing as Christians that choose to live by the Spirit? We should be helping our fellow brothers and sisters in Christ. That's what the Bible says!

If one of them becomes tangled up in sin, we should help them get their junk together. Verse 6: 1 says do it gently as if 'roughly' is the negative approach. The one thing that comes to mind is how some Christian folks like to 'finger point'. That's the wrong way.

These verses also tells us to be careful. We may think we are doing the right thing in joining them in their sin in order to help them get out of it. The next thing we know, we're being tempted by the same things. If we're not careful, we'll be in the same pit.

It's like going mudbogging and having a buddy stuck in the mud. Instead of joining him in the mud to get him out, it's best to have our tires firmly planted on dry ground first.

We're all going to have problems in life. Many of those problems are hard to deal with alone. We're all going to need some help sometimes. As brothers and sisters in Christ, we should help carry those burdens. Work through them together. That's how the body of Christ works – different parts, same body. Ya know?

It's about 'sowing' good deeds with the right heart. If we decide to help someone, we should test our actions. Why are we doing what we do? Is it for selfish reasons or are we helping them out of love? That's the difference between sowing for the sinful nature and sowing for the Spirit. The sinful nature leads to destruction and the Spirit leads to life. Keep in mind, we'll reap what we sow.

If you do good for someone out of love for them and God, it'll be life changing for that person and anyone around them. It could lead to someone getting saved or restoring their faith. If you do good only for a pat on the back or to boost your egotistical pride, people will see through it and it won't have a spiritual purpose. Yeah, you might look good and your head will swell. But remember, pride comes before the fall.

Always do good to all people, especially to those in the body of Christ. One day we will reap a harvest for the things we have done. So, never give up!

Not Circumcision but a New Creation
Galatians 6: 11-18

Verse 11 is sorta funny. It seems Paul chose to write in big letters. It may have been so that he could get a major point across to the church in Galatia. Or he decided to do some cool graffiti on a scroll and wanted them to check it out, but I seriously doubt it.

Back in these days, the proof of your faith was determined by the skin (or the lack of skin) around your genitalia. This was a serious  thing during the time of Paul and now, in present day, it seems kind of funny that it even mattered. But circumcision was their outward expression of their faith.

Paul wanted to share with them that 'being circumcised' didn't mean anything. Yeah, it told the world they were all religious and junk on the outside, but it was the condition of the heart on the inside that mattered. That's where 'being a Christian' takes root. If the heart is right, then it will manifest itself outwardly.

Folks can be all 'holy looking' on the outside, yet lost and dying in their sins. But, the day we got saved began a new creation from the inside out.

The Book Of
Ephesians

The Book Of Ephesians

Introduction To Ephesians

The book of Ephesians was written by Paul as a letter to the church in Ephesus around A.D. 60 while he was in prison in Rome. I'm sure sitting in a jail cell gave him some time to think about stuff. I would bet that he had a lot of free time to get his prayer on and talk to God.

This church in Ephesus was started by Paul in one of his missionary journeys around the globe – or at least in his neck of the woods. History tells us that it was established around A.D. 53 and Timothy served as their leader. This letter was sent to this church by a fella named Tychicus. Paul may have called him 'Ty' for short because saying his full name is sorta hard to pronounce.

Ephesians offers encouragement and strength to Christians everywhere and doesn't really confront any issues the church was having. It's a positive message that all of us can apply to our lives. My hope is that we can get something from it.

Ya'll ready to get started? Grab your Bibles and follow along with me. This is going to be fun and spiritually educational and junk.

Spiritual Blessings in Christ
Ephesians 1: 1-14

As Christians, we're blessed. I know many times it seems we're dealt the shortest straw, especially when the folks around us seem to be prospering. Many of those people that live life the way they want to seem to have it all – all the stuff that we don't. Right? How are we blessed?

To answer this question, we have to realize that blessings aren't always financial. These verses tell us that we are blessed, as Christians, with every 'spiritual' blessing from God and even gives us a little insight as to what they are:

We are adopted as His sons (verse 5)
For the record, our spiritual nature makes us enemies of God, but because of what Jesus did on the cross and our choice to receive His free gift of eternal life, we are now part of God's family.

We are redeemed and forgiven of the junk (sin) in our lives (verse 7)

Sin is what separates us from God. Jesus shed His blood on the cross, so that we can be forgiven. As Christians, we are redeemed because we are no longer slaves to sin. It's a win-win situation because we are reunited with God thanks to Jesus.

We know the mystery of His will (verse 9)
God had a purpose for sending Jesus to die for our sins (John 3:16). This is His salvation plan for humanity. A lot of folks don't understand it, but we do. There will come a time when God will call His children home together under Christ. I am thankful for being on the team. Aren't you?

We are heirs to God's estate (verse 11)
As adopted kids, we are heirs to the things that God owns. What exactly does God own? Let's just say that He owns everything. If you can see it, He owns it. If you can touch it or smell it, it's His. He's the Creator and holds a heavenly patent on everything. That's pretty cool!

We are sealed with the Holy Spirit (verse 13)
The day we got saved, God placed His Holy Spirit within us. This is

a deposit guaranteeing us of our inheritance and eternal life that He promised us.

Yeah, these blessings might not get you a fancy wardrobe or put you behind the wheel of a cool looking sports car. But, those type of things are temporary and will eventually rot and end up in a landfill somewhere. As Christians, we are given some great spiritual blessings that are extremely valuable. We should thank Him daily for them.

The cool thing that stands out to me from these verses is that we are chosen. He knew we would become part of the family before we were even created. Does this mean that God only selected a few folks to take part of His eternal plan? Does this mean that God shows favoritism to only a small portion of mankind? No! I believe He knew who would accept Him before they were even put on this Earth and everyone is given the opportunity. And those that don't, He knew they wouldn't.

Thanksgiving and Prayer
Ephesians 1: 15-23

Paul prayed for the church in Ephesus to know God better. Imagine that! How do we get to know someone better? Yeah, we could read a biography on them or maybe ask someone that knows them, but do we really know them from a few facts? We could do a little research and put their name in a search engine on the internet and it might pull up some information. Some of it might be true and there might be some details that just ain't right. But, in all honesty, we won't really know them until we spend a little time with them ourselves.

I really didn't know my wife until I married her. I look back on the times we dated and realized this girl I married had a little more details that I didn't know about. At first glance, she was the sweet and shy type full of smiles and twinklings in her eye and junk. But, when we married I saw a side of her that I've learned not to provoke again. I also got to see the sensitive side that loves me no matter how stupid I act. But, I wouldn't have known this had I not gotten to know her better. You see what I'm saying?

The same is true about God. People may share their own details with you about Him. You might even do a cool Bible study and take notes. You might even do a deep theological research and get all the books from the library on the subject and use a yellow highlighter. I mean, that's all cool and all, but you won't really know Him better unless you pray to Him and spiritually walk with Him like the disciples did. That's personal!

Paul also prayed that they would open their eyes and see the hope we have. He's not talking about the kind of hope that means life and the future is all about pink butterflies and dancing kangaroos. It's knowing that we have victory through God. We belong to God, who created the universe and runs the show. He has full control of everything that's going on around us. He has everything under His feet. There is nothing impossible for God. Knowing that should help you breathe better!

Made Alive in Christ

Ephesians 2: 1-10

It is by His grace that we are saved.

Before we accepted Jesus as Lord and Savior, we lived a life that God didn't approve of. This life of sin made us objects of God's wrath. We were considered dead in our transgressions and sin. But, because of our faith in Jesus and God's grace, we are made right in His sight and made alive.

The salvation plan is simple. There's no special work we

have to do to earn it, it's free for us to take. God loves us so much that He made it easy. He 'graciously' offered us an escape plan from our sin through Jesus Christ. It is by His grace that we are saved. You see how the whole 'grace' thing works?

These verses talks about 'rulers of the air' and 'ways of the world'. There is so much spiritual stuff that goes on in the world today that we may not see or realize that's going on. There are demonic forces actively working. I know that sounds like a B-rated horror flick, but it's true. Yeah, people's heads may not be spinning around or you may not be spewing green puke, but there's evil junk going on around us. The sad thing is that we may be involved in it without knowing. Or we are taking part in things that goes against what God is all about. This is sin!

The only way to know for sure is to read the Bible and compare notes. If you are living a life of sin, you are dead. You should accept the free gift of eternal life that God offers through Jesus.

Follow Him if you want to live!

One in Christ
Ephesians 2: 11-22

Back in the day, there were basically two types of people. You were either a Jew or a Gentile.

Being a Jew was a good thing because you got all the cool benefits that God offered as long as you did everything expected from you according to the law. This included the Ten Commandments and a list of additional laws that God gave Moses to jot down. You also had to do the proper sacrifices of animals and stuff based on the type of sin you committed. As part of your religious ceremonial practices, you had to do some sacrificial offerings of various things like wheat, oats, and an occasional corn cob every now and then.

Being a Gentile wasn't a good thing to be and was frowned on by all the cool Jews. If you were a Gentile, you were garbage.

According to this scripture, you weren't even given citizenship in Israel. You were basically a drifter without a home. And if that wasn't enough, you were also separated from God.

The funny thing to me about being either a Jew or a Gentile was the way a person could tell which one you were. It was by your 'circumcision status'. If your taddy-whacker had skin hanging on it, you were a Gentile. And if it was surgically removed during some point in your life, you were a Jew. I just wonder how folks knew for sure without playing Show-N-Tell. But, that's their business and I don't really want to know how they did it.

The key here is that being a Gentile wasn't a good thing. But, because of the blood of Jesus and Him dying on the cross, a Gentile can now be united with God. The barrier is gone. His death got rid of the law with its commandments and rules. Jews and Gentiles are joined together as one in Christ. This relationship is now built on faith in Jesus and not based on following a bunch of laws.

From verse 22, we read an important message. We, as Christians, are being built together to become a dwelling in which God lives by His Spirit. This means we are the body – we are the church. We may think of church as a building; a place where a bunch of folks get together and hear 'Jesus stuff'. But, it's not. If you think about church buildings with all of it's divided denominations, which ones would God dwell in? I believe God intended for unity of all believers – one church built together of people of one mind and one accord. Satan divided it (many years in the works) and now look at the 'church' today. It's messed up!

Paul the Preacher to the Gentiles
Ephesians 3: 1-13

Can you imagine how the Jews treated Paul knowing that he had been preaching Jesus to all those nasty cooty-infested Gentiles? He became a prisoner for it and the Jews put him

there.

Paul was sharing a mystery to the church in Ephesus that he had been preaching to others. This mystery was about God's grace. It told of how God offered, through the Gospel, that the Gentiles shared in the same inheritance as the Jews. In God's eyes, Jews and Gentiles were one and were heirs to the promise in Jesus Christ. I wonder how the Jews handled this tidbit of information. I bet it came as a shock and might of made some of them angry.

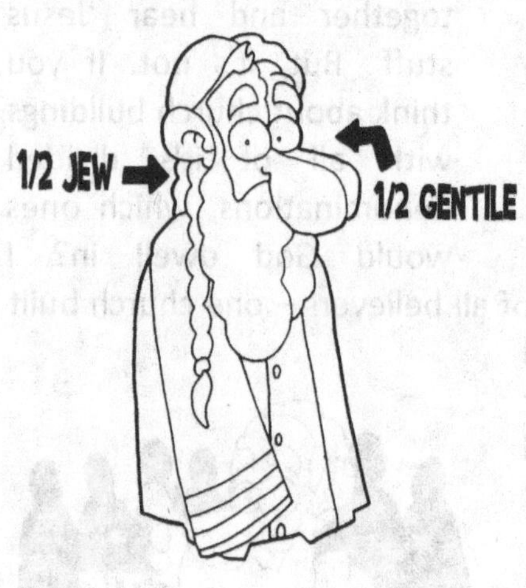

To put that in today's world, it would be like telling someone that's been going to church twice a week that God loves the drug addict on the street just the same. Or telling the lady that plays the piano during church services and teaches Sunday school that God loves the hopeless prostitute the same. By God's grace, we all have an equal opportunity to accept Jesus Christ as Lord and Savior. It's by faith in Jesus that we can approach Him with freedom and confidence. It's by faith in Him, not works for Him! It's an equal playing field. God's grace and love is for everyone.

A Prayer for the Ephesians
Ephesians 3: 14-21

These few verses is Paul's prayer for the church at Ephesus. He prayed for God to give them strength and power through His

Spirit. Why? What would they need power and strength for? I mean, they were a church that probably congregated a few times a week. What would they do with this power and strength? Move church pews?

Paul was referring to 'spiritual' power and strength and he knew they would need it to be effective for God. Satan loves churches and would love to tear one apart. Sometimes I wonder if Satan shows up to church before we do. There's been many times I have wondered if he didn't ride with us in the minivan to get there. You know what I'm talking about?

We should pray a prayer like this every day; asking the Lord to give us strength to accomplish what He would want us to do with our life. There are so many distractions that can take our minds off of Him. We need the Spirit living within us to guide us and keep us going in the right direction. We can't do this thing called 'life' on our own. Yes, we may try, but we're going to mess things up.

To be effective in ministry, we need the Spirit to tell us what to do, what to say, how to act, and to show us where we're going. It would be flictarded to think we can do the Lord's work in our own strength. The lives around us won't change and we can't lead them to the Lord if the Spirit doesn't lead us first. That power and strength comes from the Lord.

Paul's prayer was also for the Ephesians to know God's love and to be rooted in it. He even used a geometric equation: length x width x height. This is like a cubic measurement that we should fill with God's love. It may be hard for us to understand how much He loves us. Paul even says it goes beyond our ability to understand it.

The only love that I can understand is the love I have for my wife, my kids, and my parents. But to be loved beyond what I can understand must be some serious sho' 'nuff love. Know what I'm saying? God loves us a lot!

Unity In The Body Of Christ
Ephesians 4: 1-16

Paul encourages the Ephesians to live their life worthy of the calling that was given to them. He gave them the 'heads up' on Christian living and how to live in peace with the people around them. This is directed towards us, too:

- Be humble
- Be gentle

- Be patient
- Live in peace with one another in love

Paul preached 'unity' and God is cool with that. As Christians, we should unite as one because, according to this scripture, we have:

- 1 Body
- 1 Spirit
- 1 Hope
- 1 Lord
- 1 Faith
- 1 Baptism
- 1 God and Father of all

That's a lot of 1's! So why do we have so many church denominations? That's a little something to ponder on.

Verse 7 talks of Jesus as one who ascended higher than all heavens and descended to the lower parts of the Earth. When you first read this, you see that 'heaven' has an S at the end of it and it makes you wonder if there aren't several of them up there somewhere. Then your mind gets to wondering:

"I sure hope I go to the 'heaven' that my loved ones are at after I'm dead and gone."

"Dang! I bet I'll get stuck in the 'heaven' where my mother-in-law is at!"

And what about the line from verse 9 that talks about the lower parts of the Earth? I mean, we're walking on the Earth with the sand between our toes. You reckon there's a lower part? Ooh! That just sounds creepy!

But, you know, I think what it's telling us is that, by Jesus going 'up and down' Heaven and Earth, He's Lord over it all. Science has proven that there is more in the sky than just stars, moon, and the sun. There's a universe, and before long, scientists will soon find other cool stuff. But, guess what? Jesus is Lord over that, too. I guess the point is that we shouldn't concern ourselves of the location of where 'hell' and 'heaven' are. We don't know where either of them are. If we did, some oil tycoon would try to rob it of it's natural resources. Just know that Jesus is Lord and we should be more concerned with Earthly matters. That should keep us busy for a while.

Verse 11 tells us that it was He that gave certain folks the job duties of apostles, prophets, evangelists, pastors, and teachers. Their job? According to verse 12, it is to prepare God's people for works of service to build up the body of Christ. Our goal is to reach unity in the faith and in the knowledge of Jesus and to become mature as Christians. That's basically what it's all about right there.

If you're a teacher, teach folks about Jesus and help them grow. Pastors should preach the Gospel and allow the Spirit to use them to win souls for Jesus. Everything we should do for the Lord should be about Him and helping baby Christians grow and walk in the faith. That's good stuff!

Living as Children of Light
Ephesians 4: 17-32, 5: 1-21

Paul tells the church in Ephesus to not live like the Gentiles did with their wrong way of thinking and hardened hearts towards God. I wonder why the Gentiles were this way. You would think they would be excited to know that they had hope for their sinful nature in Jesus. But then again, they may have seen how the 'holier than thou' Jews acted towards them and thought, "If this is what being a Christian is all about, I don't want any part of it."

The Gentiles didn't know God. All they knew about God was what they saw in the Jews and how they lived their life and treated them. What are the 'lost' seeing in us as Christians? Is it a life that leads them to Jesus? Do we reflect the One that saved us? Or do we treat people that don't know Him as if we're spraying them with cooty spray?

One thing we can be sure of is that a life separated from God is an uncertain road that can take you anywhere. Many times it's places you will not want to be. There are so many temptations that can take your life down dirt roads without caution signs that eventually run you off a cliff. That's why we need God in our life. Even as Christians, we need to put aside our old sinful nature and put on the new self, which is created to be like Jesus.

Paul gives the Ephesians some helpful tips to live by and we should apply these to our lives, too:

- Always speak the truth when dealing with folks

- When we get mad, don't sin and don't stay angry

- Quit stealing, instead do something useful

- Watch your mouth and stop talking trash

- Don't grieve the Holy Spirit — by rebelling and doing the things you know you shouldn't

- Get rid of bitterness, rage and anger, brawling and slander, and every form of malice.

- Instead, be kind, compassionate, and forgiving towards others

This is how we as Christians should live as children of the Light. By being imitators of Jesus and how He lived, we are able to live a life of love that folks will take notice of. And people are watching.

Paul continues in Chapter 5 with some additional helpful tips for Christian living. Don't look at it as a list of Do's and Don'ts and get all crazy thinking that being a Christian is about following lists. It's not! It's like a home improvement project, and since the Holy Spirit is dwelling within you, give Him something cozy to live in. Put some paint on the walls. Replace the carpet and do some mopping. You know it needs it. Here are some of Paul's home improvement tips for better living:

Get rid of:

- Any sexual immorality (even the stuff we think is small and insignificant)

- Any kind of impurity

- Greed

223

- Obscenity, foolish talk,
  or coarse joking

It's all about living as children of the Light. Before God saved us, we were living in darkness. Not only does this 'shiny' way of living please the Lord, it also benefits us. When we live for Jesus, life is lived more peacefully and a lot of the stressful headaches go away. Just sayin'.

Wives and Husbands
Ephesians 5: 22-33

I honestly can't understand how people can take these verses and flip-flop it around to mean that a man should be a dictator towards his wife. It don't add up! It's like they read it and stop at 'the husband is the head of the wife' and then fill in the rest with their own thoughts about it. That ain't cool!

Marriage is a spiritual partnership that God puts together. It's a team of two – a man and a woman – working together under Christ. He should be the foundation that this marriage sits on. These verses compares marriage to how Jesus is with the church. He sacrificed His life for it. As men, we should be the head of our homes and we should be willing to sacrifice ourselves for our wives. We should love them as much as Jesus loves the church. That's what these verses tell us. If we want to be the husbands that God wants us to be, we can learn from the example that

Jesus gave.

The woman's role in this partnership should be to be submissive to their husbands in everything and respect them. The example is in how the church submits to Christ. Sometimes this involves putting aside our interests for the sake of the man you love.

A great marriage is when both people are living for the Lord. With Jesus in our marriage, He teaches us the proper way to love one another and how to treat each other. This spiritual partnership can only grow stronger when Jesus is leading the way. Ya know?

Children and Parents

Ephesians 6: 1-4

"Children, obey your parents!"

Parenting is cool and I think it's entertaining to have a few rugrats running around the house. From the day those little boogers popped out, it has been a joy. That is, until they were able to talk. That is when the real fun begins.

I believe it is in our human nature to automatically rebel and go against the system. When our kids were babies, they were all cute and all. But then they learned how to walk and use their little baby arms and legs. Then they started learning to talk and say cute little things. But somewhere and somehow along the line they began using these newly developed skills to get on our nerves by doing stupid stuff. It's like, "Whoa! What happened to that sweet innocent little cutey pie that we brought home from the hospital?"

At this point, real parenting begins. It's up to us to get these kids prepared for the real world and we have a few short years to do it. For some of us, parenting lasts beyond the teenage years. But, that's a different story.

In the first three verses, Paul is talking to the kids about how they should obey their parents. Not only is it the right thing to do, but it comes with a promise of being able to enjoy a longer life. Did he mean that obedient kids live longer because God will extend their lifespan? Or that their risk of being choked to death by their parents decreases? Either way, it seem that there is a benefit for kids that listen to what their parents say.

Parenting is tough. No doubt! But it's easier when we are raising them up in a Godly home. As Christian parents following the Lord, the values we're taught of being forgiving, caring, and love will make things easier in raising our kids up right. Love should always be the motive for discipline, not anger. Right?

And kids, obey your parents. For real! You should make things easier on them. Quit rebelling against them and listen to them for a change. They're looking out for you and want what's best for you. Remember, before your parents were old and wrinkly, they were just like you and probably went through the same stuff you're going through. They have already learned the life lessons and are wanting to prevent you from going through the same junk. Listen to them.

Slaves and Masters

Ephesians 6: 5-9

Slavery was part of the culture back in the day when Paul wrote this letter to the church in Ephesus. I mean, it was just how it was. I know that in today's world, 'slavery' is an ugly word and has created a bad picture of a life that nobody wants to see again. But, to be honest with ourselves, slavery is still alive and well in society today. It's just called something different. It's called 'being employed' or 'having a job'. I mean, would we really get out of bed to go to that place of business for the pure fun and excitement? Yeah, I didn't think so.

From these verses, we can learn some cool Christian work ethics. It teaches us as employees how we should act in our jobs. It also teaches our bosses how to treat us as employees. In God's eyes we're both on the same playing level, but on Earth it shares some wisdom on how to 'get along' in the workplace.

As employees, we should respect our bosses and obey them as we would Jesus. We shouldn't do it to get brownie points with the hopes of getting moved up the corporate ladder. But, we should work wholeheartedly and sincere as if we were serving the Lord. God rewards those that do good. It could be with a job promotion or with a bonus attached to your weekly check. The key is here is to do your job and think of it as being employed by Jesus Himself.

For the big chiefs in charge, treat your employees fair. You don't have to strut around the office with your nose in the air looking down on folks. What would Jesus do? Learn from His example.

It's all about working together in peace and harmony.

The Armor of God
Ephesians 6: 10-20

As a Christian, have you ever thought of yourself as a soldier in a mighty army? It's not that we are 'super special and junk'. It's because we are serving a Mighty God with several others on the same battlefield. There's a war going on. Even though we may not see it, it's on like a chicken bone! It's a spiritual war and Satan is the General on the opposite side.

That's why these verses tell us to put on the full armor of God. If it were a physical war, we could load up on some shotguns, ammo, and drive around in an armored tank and be all right. But this thing is spiritual and those things just won't protect you. You have to gear up spiritually.

What should we be totin'? Paul tells us to put on:

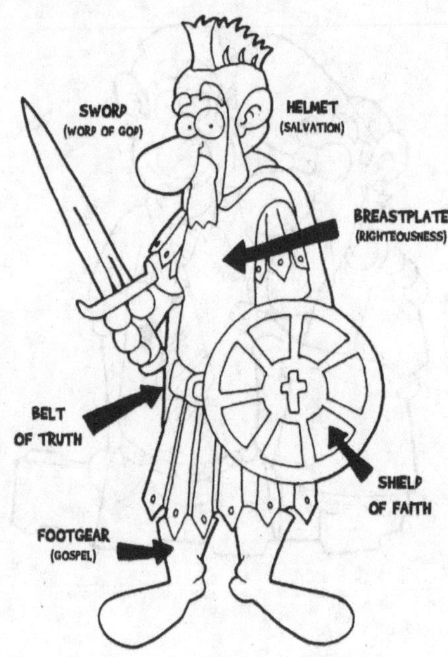

The belt of truth around our waist
This is the knowledge of the truth of God's Word. It's hard to fight a spiritual war without knowing what the Bible says. You have to read it for yourself.

The breastplate of righteousness
This is living a holy life in character and in moral conduct. We should strive to live like Jesus every day.

The gospel of peace on our feet
We should be ready and willing to share the Good News of Jesus Christ anywhere and at any time.

The shield of faith
This is where we reach the point where we can take God at His word and believe in His promises. This will protect us from the flaming arrows that Satan shoots at us. Believe me, he will shoot them.

The helmet of Salvation
This is the assurance of your Salvation – knowing that you know that you know without a doubt that you are saved.

The sword of the Spirit
This is the Word of God. Read it, think on it, study it, plant that sucka in your heart. This is what you're fighting back with.

We should always be praying spiritually with all kinds of requests, especially praying for the others that are fighting with you on the battlefield. The battle's on!

Final Greetings

Ephesians 6: 21-24

Paul ends his letter to the church at Ephesus with a final greeting of peace, love, and grace. He also sends to them a fellow servant and brother in Christ, Tychicus.

Tychicus is mentioned a few times in the Bible: Acts 20: 4, Colossians 4: 7, 2 Timothy 4: 12, and Titus 3: 12. His purpose was to keep the church informed on how Paul was doing in his ministry and to keep the church encouraged.

Being a Christian serving in ministry or just being a Christian in general has times of discouragement. Yep! That's right! It's easy to get down and out when we are faced with struggles and problems. Many times it seems we are all alone and that nobody cares.

But, you know what's cool? God sends people in our life for the simple purpose of just lifting us up and keeping us focused on Jesus. At that time, when we have lost hope, someone pops up in our life and says the right thing to keep us going. That's amazing to me.

We're not alone in this world. God cares! He is always actively working ahead of us to get us the spiritual help we need when we need it. People that encourage one another are gifts from God.

As Christians, we should be willing to let God use us to lift folks up. A simple word of encouragement goes a long way. We should

call someone today or pray with them. Look for people that may need to hear something positive from you. Be that vessel for God to use to keep His people motivated and moving.

I could only hope that I have been an encouragement to someone. We're all on the same team working together for the same goals. Each of us has a role to play in the Lord's work here on Earth. We need to be a light to folks out there. Ya know?

The Book Of
Philippians

The Book Of Philippians

Introduction To Philippians

What does it mean to be happy? I reckon 'being happy' would be having a life of luxury; being able to buy anything we want or go anywhere in the world whenever we want with a simple swipe of our debit card. I mean, we're happy because the money is actually in our bank account and we're not using credit to do it. That would be pretty awesome, wouldn't it?

Happiness could be having great health. For some of us, we know it ain't all about the money. We're smarter than that because we know we can't enjoy the money if we're unhealthy lying up in a hospital somewhere.

How about being able to accumulate stuff? Does that make you happy? If you were like me several years ago, you know what it's like to find bargains. It's hard to pass up. It could be a discounted item at Home Depot or Lowe's. Or it could be some cool stuff you found at a really low price at a yard sale. If it was a deal, we bought it and brought it home and stuffed it in with our other cool stuff that we have found.

Before long, we got a garage full of stuff. Yeah, we may not use it, but knowing we have it is all that matters. And that makes us happy, right?

What about having 'smart' kids? Does that make you happy? I've learned to 'compromise' in this area and just be happy with the ones I got. None of them have made honor roll at school or even got a certificate for being the brightest crayon in the box, but that's alright. My kids make me happy and I kinda like 'em a lot.

But, what happens when this 'happiness' is gone? When the bank account dries up? The stuff gets old and rusty or breaks? And the kids get older and move away? It seems that happiness then turns to despair. We're left with this lonely depressed feeling and we're all sad and junk.

There's another word that is similar to happiness. It is called 'joy'. Ever heard of that one? It's not just a brand of dish washing liquid. It's an actual feeling that we, as humans, can express. It runs deeper than happiness and is usually stronger. It's a quiet, confident feeling knowing that God loves us, and that He is working in our lives. With joy, you have confidence knowing that He will always be there no

matter what life throws at you. This will make you content in any situation.

Happiness depends on 'what's happenin'', but joy depends on Jesus. Big difference, huh?

Philippians was a letter that Paul wrote to the Christians living in Philippi around A.D. 61. I don't have a clue where Philippi is, but I have read that it's somewhere in Europe. It was the first church established there. The cool thing is that this letter was written while Paul was in prison in Rome. Poor fella! He was always getting himself in some kind of trouble by sharing the Gospel. I guess some important folks didn't want to hear it.

Personally, I'm curious of what's in here. I hope you are, too. You will need to get your Bible and follow along with me. If yours is dusty, go ahead and dust it off with one of them fuzzy sticks so that you can breathe better. It's sorta hard to read when you're all sneezing and junk.

The Book of Philippians... four chapters! It should be an easy read, but we can guarantee there will be some cool stuff in it for us.

Thanksgiving and Prayer
Philippians 1: 1-11

Paul addresses this letter to the saints, overseers and the deacons. For the record, saints are the folks that believe in Jesus. If you are saved today, you are considered a saint according to the Bible. Now I wouldn't go around adding that title to your name because that would look all weird and junk to the people we socialize with. But, just know that in God's big family, we are all considered important and can be used by Him to do some great things. As a saint, we can hold our heads up and walk boldly as 'saints of God'. That's something to feel good about.

Overseers and deacons were job titles within the church. Overseers were bishops and pastors. Deacons weren't the gray-haired fellas that would fall asleep on the first pew during services. They actually had church responsibilities. They all had the job of looking out for the church and the folks that attended. You can check out their responsibilities and qualifications by reading 1 Timothy 3: 1-13 to get more information. It was a big deal and should be today for a church to run smoothly.

In prayer, Paul would thank God for the folks in Philippi. He was glad to know that they were serious about sharing the Gospel like he was. This gave him joy.

In ministry, sometimes it seems like we're the only ones 'on fire' trying to share the Gospel with others. In our churches, it may seem like you're the only one doing something for the Lord. Even though this may be true in the church you're working in, the 'box' is much bigger in the spiritual world. There are others doing the same thing all over the world. That should be encouraging to know. 'Team Jesus' is made up of believers (all over the place) that share the same passion

as you do. Your 'solo project' may be where you're at now, but on the big playing field, you have team members that are actively working hard like you are. Knowing that should pump you up with joy.

When you feel like you're alone in ministry, discouragement can set in and cause you to sit still. I mean, it looks like everyone else is 'doing nothing' so why shouldn't you, right? We have to look outside the box on a bigger scale. We need to get excited about what we're doing for the Lord. Your 'joy' could be what it takes to get those around you on fire.

Paul encourages the Philippians by letting them know that God, who began this good work in them, will finish it. God doesn't give up on us. If He starts something in us, He will see it through.

In ministry, God is using us to do some cool stuff for Him. We are His tools to make it happen. Yes, we will get discouraged from time to time, but God will send the right people to keep us motivated. He takes the time to train us and grow us to be useful for His glory. That's pretty awesome!

For the record, anything we do for the glory of God is considered ministry work. If it's walking around sharing your testimony to people, that's ministry. If it's teaching a Sunday School class to a bunch of wired-up kindergartners, that's ministry. If you're preaching to a maxed out congregation, that's ministry. Just know, everything in ministry is equally important to God. Bunch of parts... one body!

Paul's Chains Advance the Gospel
Philippians 1: 12-30

Keep in mind that Paul is writing this big ol' letter in prison. He was in the 'chain gang' folks! Think about it. Paul, a changed man called to share the Gospel to the world, is sitting in a jail cell. How is he gonna do his God-called job hanging out with a bunch of smelly Roman jailers and prisoners? You would think his ministry failed. It's over! God must be punishing him for doing such a bad job! Oh well, maybe Paul can just spend the rest of his life watching Camel TV and working out with some weights in the prison gym. He could also play some cards with the fellas and maybe read some books that the prison guards gave him. The whole ministry thing's done! Or was it?

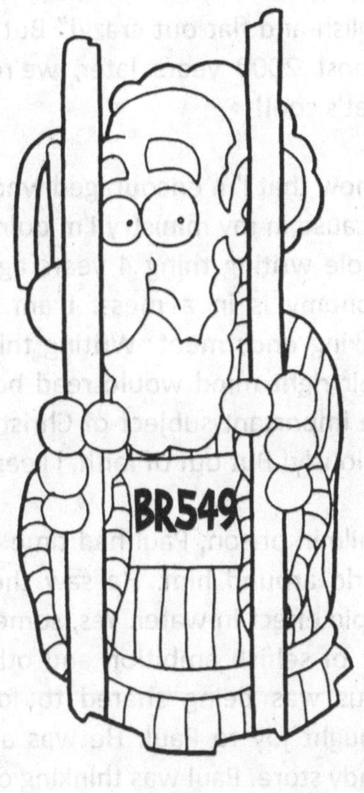

He obviously had a feathery pen, some ink, and a scroll. He also loved people and wanted to keep them encouraged in the Great Commission of sharing Jesus with folks. So, he put those pieces together and wrote letters. In today's world, he would be considered a mega-blogger. Can you imagine what he would've done with a laptop and a high speed internet connection?

There may have been many times that Paul got discouraged. He may have wondered, "Why am I sitting in this jail cell when the world needs to know about Jesus? Instead, I'm sitting here just writing letters to folks that may not even read them. Man, this is foolish and flat-out crazy!" But, he kept on keepin' on! And now almost 2000 years later, we're still reading his letters! Wow! That's cool!

I know that I'm encouraged when I read them. I can relate to Paul because in my ministry I'm doing something similar. I started this whole writing thing 4 years ago not knowing the purpose. The economy is in a mess. I am unemployed and we are barely making ends meet. Writing this stuff seems ridiculous! Who in their right mind would read books written by a simple man on the important subject of Christianity? Who would care? I mean, seriously! But out of faith, I keep pressing on.

While in prison, Paul had time to think. He was able to view the world around him. He saw the Gospel move outward like the ripple effect in water. Yes, some folks were preaching the Gospel out of selfish ambition and other motives, but it didn't matter. Jesus was being shared to folks that didn't know Him. This brought joy to Paul. He was all happy and junk like a kid in a candy store. Paul was thinking outside of the box.

Paul's view of life was 'to live' and 'to die'. For him, either one was for Jesus. While he was kickin', he could live for Jesus. If he died, he would meet Him. So, it didn't matter to him because it was a win-win situation.

We should have that same attitude in life. Regardless of our situation, struggles or financial position in life, just live it for the Lord. We are where God has us! We should make the best of it for Jesus. We can't spend time worrying about folks doing 'Jesus stuff' for their own personal gain. That's between them and God. We should make sure we're doing what the Bible tells us to do. We can encourage folks like Paul did, and most importantly, we should be doing what God has called us to do. Our life has a deadline date. While we're living, serve the Lord and lead others to Him. And after we're dead, we will have eternity to hang out and chill with Him. I'm looking forward to it!

Imitating Christ's Humility

Philippians 2: 1-11

Paul tells the Philippians that their attitude should be the same as the attitude that Jesus had. This would involve loving people and not doing things out of selfish ambition. Having humility and a servant spirit would be His characteristics.

That sounds like an easy change – a little overnight Jekyll and Hyde transformation, right? Wrong.

The day we chose to follow Jesus and live for Him, we embarked on a journey that began changing our lives. For some of us it may have seemed like everything was going downhill. Things in our life started getting rearranged. For example, if you were financially secure before, you may have lost some material stuff or been put in a situation where you had to ask someone for help. Or maybe your first assignment as a Christian was to help minister to people in need like the homeless. It's through spiritual exercises like these that we learn what it means to be humble. It helps remove any selfishness we may have had before. Our life begins transforming into a life of thinking about other people first.

246

Unfortunately, many people give up during this training process and miss out on living the kind of life that Jesus shared with us – a life that leads others.

Jesus set the example folks. He humbled himself to become a servant. He loved people and even died for them.

"No greater love hath no man than to lay down His life for His friends." I think that's how that scripture goes.
We need to strive to be like Him.

Shining As Stars
Philippians 2: 12-18

This church in Philippi were a good group of folks. They were doing the things they were supposed to and living right. That's awesome! And then there's this verse about 'working out their salvation'. It sounds as if their salvation depended on their works and great deeds. Or that in order to stay saved, they had to 'work at it'. That just doesn't sound right.

We know from previous books of the Bible that salvation is a gift from God. It's free for the askin'. We are saved by faith not works. Remember that? So, what's this whole 'working out our salvation' thing?

Let's say our bodies get all flabby and junk due to lack of exercise. How do you get it in shape? You work it out! Salvation comes with some cool outward changes as long as you let it. We become more and more like Jesus the more we put our faith into practice. God works in us and helps us do great things for His glory when we allow Him. To grow as Christians, it's about putting our salvation on a treadmill. Put it to work! Work it out! Great things will happen.

Whiners and complainers. It seems every church has them. They are usually the ones that are never happy with the way things in the church are run. To them, the thermostat on the air conditioner is never set to the right temperature. It's either too hot or too cold. They forget that many churches out there are still using the paper fans on a stick. They should be thankful.

When it comes to helping the church serve the community,

they rarely do it. And if they do, they'll fuss about it instead of focusing on the people in need. And you can also spot the whiner and complainer because they are usually the ones with the stopwatch that puts a timer on the preacher. That's not cool.

So, what's wrong with having a whiner and complainer in the church? Well, for one, it causes a ruckus among the folks that go there. This attitude makes people leave. Plus, it flat out makes the church and its purpose in the community look bad. It leaves a bad impression. Who wants to go to a church like that? I don't.

As a church, it should shine bright in the community it's in – a beacon for everyone to see. It should be a safe place where they can find the Lord, not a bunch of whiners and complainers. They can find that at a bar.

Timothy and Epaphroditus
Philippians 2: 19-30

Two fellas – Timothy and Epaphroditus. Paul felt a need to call these fellas out in these verses. Timothy was a young apprentice in the ministry field. He and his father were part of Paul's ministry team. Since Paul was in prison, he trusted Timothy with his job duties because he knew that he had the passion for it. He cared about folks and looked out for their best interest. This is a main ingredient in discipleship.

You have to have the right heart in doing the Lord's work. If your heart ain't in it, you might as well stay at home. This means actually caring about people and looking out for their best interest. We live in a world where it seems everyone is looking out for themselves. This includes some ministries and church people. We should share Timothy's enthusiasm in serving and doing God's work.

Epaphroditus was sent to Paul by the church in Philippi to help him. Unfortunately, the fella got very sick and almost died in the line of duty. It appears that Paul needed some serious help from a few of their church members and they only sent him one person. Poor Epap was trying to carry the load. Paul saw fit that the Philippians should honor him when he returned for his dedication and service.

As a church, we should honor those that go out into the field to serve God. There are missionaries whose purpose is to travel to other places in order to share the Gospel. Sometimes they go to dangerous places where they are risking their lives. These special people are willing to go where some of us wouldn't. These people deserve our recognition and we should be willing to freely support the stuff they do.

No Confidence in the Flesh
Philippians 3: 1-11

Paul was telling the Philippians to watch out for the Jews that tried to push their religion off on them. They tried to talk 'em into getting circumcised, following their traditional laws and that this was the only way to God. These Jews had a problem believing that salvation was a free gift through Jesus. That's why Paul gave them a warning to watch out. Them Jews were tricky.

251

If a Christian person isn't firmly rooted in their faith in Jesus, it's easy to follow any religion that 'seems right'. This person needs to read the Bible for themselves and allow the Holy Spirit to teach them what it says so that they will know. As Christians, we can't rely on other folks teaching us and assuming they know what they're talking about. Just because they wear a suit and slick back their hair, it doesn't make them a Bible scholar. And don't be afraid to question why certain Christian religions do some of the things they do. If what they're doing is not in the Bible, stay away from it. We live in a tricky world and religion is Satan's playground. He can have you doing some weird junk and make you think that this is what it takes to be right with God. The Bible says the only way to God is through Jesus. Salvation is free. Be careful out there!

In the remaining verses, it sounds like Paul was bragging about how cool he was and junk. But, he wasn't. He was making a point. All of his accomplishments in life didn't mean anything compared to his relationship with Jesus. His new life had more meaning and purpose than anything he had ever done in his flesh. And after looking at his list of achievements, he had done some cool stuff.

For folks that don't know Jesus as their Lord and Savior, this way of thinking may be a hard pill to swallow. They may not understand how rewarding it is knowing that, as a child of God, our sins are forgiven and that we have eternal life. All of that stuff we've piled up here on Earth – our achievements, our wealth, our knowledge – it doesn't measure up. We can't take that stuff with us when we're dead. Those of us that have given our lives to Jesus and accepted His gift of salvation, we will be resurrected, just like He was, when this life is over. And we will be leaving those framed certificates behind. Just sayin'.

Pressing on Toward the Goal
Philippians 3: 12 – 4: 1

As Christians, we are continuously growing as long as we devote time to the Lord. This would involve prayer, studying His Word, and actually living the way Jesus wanted us to. The Holy Spirit is living within us to guide us in the right direction. He's helping us to grow to be more like Jesus. We're not perfect, but He's helping us get there.

The more we live our lives following Jesus, the more we see our imperfections. We will always be a 'work in progress'. We shouldn't let this get us discouraged or wore out. We have to keep on keepin' on! Stay on the path! Paul was telling the folks in Phillipi to do the same.

Look at what you have learned as a Christian through every thing you've been through; the knowledge you've gained through studying God's Word; the experiences you've had while serving the Lord. Stand firm! Never forget them!

We should keep our focus on Eternity and doing what the Lord wants us to do. We shouldn't be so concerned with earthly pleasures and pushing aside our relationship with the Lord in order to get them. Our spiritual stuff is more important and valuable than the temporary earthly junk. Know what I mean?

We have an eternal home waiting for us. We don't need a passport because we already have citizenship. We're just waiting for the Jesus Express to come pick us up. There will come a day when we can leave all this junk behind – our broken down bodies, the earthly stress and problems. We will be transformed! That will be an exciting day, won't it?

255

Exhortations

Philippians 4: 2-9

One of the key verses from this is the one that says, "Don't be anxious about nothing." Anxious? Anxiety, stress, worry – ya know, the stuff we do when problems pop up in our day to day lives. It basically says not to worry about it. That's easier said than done, right?

Why shouldn't we worry? Because God is in control. That doesn't mean problems won't spring up! It doesn't mean we won't face some junk from time to time! It means we shouldn't worry about it! It tells us to turn those worries into prayers with some 'thank yous'. And when we do, God will give us peace about it. You know why? Because He's in control and we gave Him our problems. We recognized that He is in charge of our life and He will work out the details.

Some folks will say, 'that's like passing the buck' or 'we're using Jesus as a crutch in life'. Well, the Bible says what it says and it tells me to hand it over to Him. However, He may decide to open some doors for us to work the problem out. When He does, we can't just sit. Here's an example:

The economy is in a mess and many families are struggling with their finances. It's hard to make ends meet. My family is right in there with them. Recently, the worst thing that could happen to a broke family happened to us. Our only vehicle decided to brake down and it needed a new motor and transmission. These two items are probably the most  expensive parts a car can get and we had to buy them. But how? We're broke! Here's where the stress comes in. We prayed about it. God didn't drop money down from Heaven. I didn't miraculously receive a check in the mail from a long lost relative that happened to be a multi-billionaire. Oh no! A door opened up to work so that we could have the money to pay for it. It required me to get off the couch and earn it. The miracle was that the door opened. God alone opened that door for me. Yes, I was stressed in the beginning, but now that I look back, I really didn't have to. He was in control.

That's what it's about right there! It's about giving Him your worries and allowing Him to handle it the way He wants to handle it. He cares about us and is looking out for us. We should do more praying about stuff instead of stressing out about it. Let's keep our minds free of those things that worry us and focus more on God and the stuff that brings us peace.

Stress has been proven to shorten our life span. It causes

wrinkles and it probably makes our hair fall out. No one wants to look like a dried up prune. God wants us to have life and to live it abundantly. That's one of the great things about being a Christian and having a Father in Heaven that loves me. He's got my back! He's in control of my life! Any problem I face, I know that I can hand it over to Him. Do you want peace like that? It's available through Jesus. Get you some!

Thanks for Their Gifts
Philippians 4: 10-23

The church in Philippi helped with Paul's ministry, even when other churches didn't. Paul was thankful. There's a scripture that says, "God loves a cheerful giver" and I believe the Philippians had the right attitude when they gave. Paul reminded them that God will continue supplying all of their needs.

What is it about money that's so cool? If we receive it, it makes us feel all good and junk. But, if we give it away, it's almost like pulling teeth. I guess money gives us a false sense of security. As long as we have a chunk of it in our bank account, we feel better about ourselves and we don't seem to worry too much. But, if we ever reach a point where we're rolling coins to make ends meet, life gets stressful. Or we get all tense when we choose to give a little to help someone. It's like we removed a few bricks from our security wall and now we're vulnerable to financial attacks.

Paul tells us that he has learned to be content in any situation – whether poor or wealthy. It didn't matter. He's experienced them both. How can a person be content being broke? I mean, I have no problem being content with a huge bank roll. But, being broke? How's that possible?

Paul reveals the secret in verse 13: *"I can do all things through Christ which strengtheneth me."*

From this verse, Paul is telling us who his power source is and that he knows God is in control. God is in control of our life, too. We have a promise that God will supply all of our needs. Do you realize how cool that is? Regardless of the economic situation of the world, we can be confident to know that God is in charge of our financial outcome. We don't have to rely on the Dow Jones stock market thing to determine if we are going to eat or not. God will supply our needs.

Learning to rely on God for everything will keep our minds off of money so that we can be content with being poor or wealthy. It won't really matter either way. We will then be living life off of God's provision and not depending on green paper and round metal. You with me? God is the power source ya'll.

The Book Of
Colossians

The Book Of Colossians

Introduction To Colossians

Have you ever went out to your truck and it wouldn't start? You walk over and lift the hood and realize the battery cables are loose on the posts. Well, we know that's a simple fix – tighten the cable ends. Right?

Let's pretend for a moment that we don't have a clue about simple mechanics. For this repair, we called our buddy Joe-Bob and told him about our car problem. He was quick to give us a solution.

"Well, if you wiggle this red thing and tap Dixie on this square metal box, it should fix your problem."

His advice didn't completely work, but the truck did make a little noise and you did begin smelling something from under the hood, so Joe-Bob must know a little something. Let's call Sally-Jane and see if she can help.

"Thanks for calling. You know, since I am highly educated in this area of expertise with my certificate hanging on my wall and junk, I have your solution. If you will open the glove box and jiggle the doo-lolly and flim-flop the doo-hatchy located directly under jimmer-jammer, it'll be as good as new."

Sally-Jane must have known what she is talking about because now the truck is running. It does, however, smoke like a freight train and sputters when we mash the gas pedal. But, it is running. Maybe one more phone call will do the trick.

You see, the church in Colosse was allowing other 'religious hoopla' to enter into their established Christian doctrine.

This was getting them all confused. Paul wrote this letter to the church to help them get their junk together.

Jesus Christ is all we need. He is our 'connection' for life. And the cool thing is, the Book of Colossians is considered a book of connections.

It was written by Paul around A.D. 60 while he was in prison in

Rome. He didn't even start the church in Colosse or had even been there before. But, God saw a need to have him write this letter to help.

I believe it's intended for us also. We might learn a little something from it. So, go get your Bible down from the shelf, dust it off, and turn to the Book of Colossians. Let's dig in and get serious with God's Word today!

Thanksgiving and Prayer
Colossians 1: 1-14

This begins as an encouraging letter to the church in Colosse. It sounds like these folks have got it all together. They have faith in Jesus and love for the saints, which is the Christian brothers and sisters. This perfect combination must be working because Paul is seeing fruits from it all around him. The gospel

was growing and that's how it's supposed to be. It grows and bears fruit when it's shared correctly.

The negative approach is to hammer 'Jesus' into people's heads until it gives them a splitting headache. They run from it because His name becomes more of a weapon. However, when you share Jesus, as God of love and compassion – the Remedy for the sins of this world, you in turn help build relationships. When folks allow Jesus to step into their lives, their hearts change for the good and begins showing outward fruit. They live better and have productive lives that, in turn, trickle down to someone else. These folks catch on and do the same. It grows and bears more fruit. That's what Paul was talking about.

Paul also prayed for these people to receive knowledge of God's will for them and for the strength to endure with patience. Take note that he didn't pray for them to receive material wealth or for bigger church attendance. He knew what was more important.

Knowledge of God's will? I believe God has a purpose for everyone. I would almost guarantee that if He didn't, they wouldn't be walking around today. To know His will would be to first get a relationship going on by accepting Jesus' free gift of salvation. Getting forgiveness of sins would be the next step because the Bible says He ain't listening when we have all them unconfessed sins weighing us down.

Our main purpose here on Earth is to serve God. You agree? I believe God prepares us with the right tools to use to serve Him. This could be our talents, gifts and experiences that He has given us or allowed us to go through. This is part of the spiritual tool box to do His will while we're here. Praying for 'knowledge of His will' would be like saying, "Lord, I'm here for You. Use me Lord and show me what I can do. I'm ready to get my hands dirty."

From experience, He'll prepare you before putting you in the battlefield. You'll go through life experiences that will train you spiritually. You'll do some sample exercises where you can use the things – talents, gifts, etc - that God has given you. You may even get to see some fruits of your labor – folks saved. That would be pretty cool, wouldn't it?

So, why did Paul pray for them to receive strength? Let's just say that 'spiritual boot camp' ain't a day in an amusement park. It can be tough, tiring, and totally terrible! In the training process, you'll go through tests and trials that will stretch your faith to it's limits — just like a rubber band. You may even give up a time or two. But, through this process, you will learn to trust and love God more and more. And when you're on the battlefield for His glory, you

will be confident knowing that He is always there with you.

Here's the scenario. You're a tool for the Lord to use to share a remedy to folks needing a cure for sin. You're walking on dangerous ground, like a mine field, with every attempt to deliver it. Satan, who is on the opposing side, doesn't want you doing it and would love to keep you away from the ones he's already trapped.

But here's the deal. Jesus came to set the captives free and can use us to deliver His remedy. Our choices are to allow Him to use us or simply set on the Christian sidelines just like so many are already doing.

The Bible says the field is ready, but the workers are few. I wonder why there's not too many workers. They may have known what God's will is and chose not to accept it. Are you one of them?

The Supremacy of Christ
Colossians 1: 15-23

Jesus... many of the Jews saw Him as the carpenter's kid from Jerusalem. As He grew older, He became more of a troublemaker for them and their religious beliefs and traditions. So, in the end, they crucified him. But, this was just the beginning of something great and was all part of God's perfect plan for humanity in restoring us back to Him. His death erased sin for those of us that believe.

These verses give us some deeper insight into who He really is.

- **He is the image of the invisible God.**

269

- **Everything on Earth and in Heaven (both visible and invisible) was created by Him and for Him**

- **He is before all things – He's number 1**

- **In Him, all things hold together – the Sustainer of life.**

- **He is head of the body and the church**

- **He is the beginning**

- **He is the firstborn of the dead**

Here's some additional scripture to tell us who Jesus really is:

- **He is equal to God**
  Who, being in the form of God, thought it not robbery to be equal with God: - Philippians 2:6

- **He is God**
  I and my Father are one. - John 10: 30

- ***He came from Heaven (not from Earth)***
  The first man is of the earth, earthy: the second man is the Lord from heaven. - 1 Corinthians 15:47

- **He's Lord over all**
  Whose are the fathers, and of whom as concerning the flesh Christ came, who is over all, God blessed for ever. Amen. - Romans 9: 5

- **He is holy**

For such an high priest became us, who is holy, harmless, undefiled, separate from sinners, and made higher than the heavens; Who needeth not daily, as those high priests, to offer up sacrifice, first for his own sins, and then for the people's: for this he did once, when he offered up himself. For the law maketh men high priests which have infirmity; but the word of the oath, which was since the law, maketh the Son, who is consecrated for evermore. - Hebrews 7: 26-28

- **He has authority to judge the world**
  In the day when God shall judge the secrets of men by Jesus Christ according to my gospel. - Romans 2: 16

Because the Bible plainly tells us the supremacy of Jesus, we can boldly confront religions that don't recognize Him as such. This would include those that say He was just a simple prophet or teacher.

How do you see Jesus today? He is more than just a carpenter's kid that talked a lot or a baby in 'waddled up' clothes born in a feeding trough.

He is God; Lord of all.

Paul's Labor for the Church

Colossians 1: 24 - 2: 5

Paul was basically an evangelistic minister sharing the Gospel with as many people as he could. He gave up his rewarding job working for the Romans as a Christian killer – which probably paid good with a fringe benefits– to pursue sharing Jesus with people for free.

He did, however, have his tent making business on the side, but the Bible doesn't say how it was doing economically. I would hope he was able to make a little bit of income from it cause the ministry suffered a lot. Only a few churches supported him financially.

Can you imagine what it would be like to do the Lord's work with an empty stomach? Paul went hungry a few times – not to mention the persecutions he received from the folks that didn't want to hear a word he had to say anyway. Poor Paul was arrested, probably knocked around a bit, and he probably could've used a new pair of sandals too with as much walking as he was doing. He went through a lot of stuff. But why? He could've turned back. But he didn't. So, why suffer?

Well, Paul loved Jesus. He received the 'love letter' that Jesus freely gives the world. He knew what His birth, death, and resurrection was all about. Paul also shared the same love for everyone that Jesus has. That was his purpose behind his ministry. He was willing to suffer for it.

Paul became a servant to everyone in order to fulfill the calling that God had placed on him. He shared the Word. His goal was to make sure the churches fully understood his message so that they weren't confused with all of the false information being passed around. He wanted everyone to be united in love with one another and Colosse had it going on.

Freedom From Human Regulations Through Life With Christ
Colossians 2: 6-23

People are always looking for something to make life better. The sad thing is that they don't include God into the equation.

Wanna feel all 'gooey' inside with happiness and junk? There are books in bookstores and libraries everywhere guaranteeing a 'better life'. Many are written by big-teethed preachers or hippie gurus that are probably missing a few brain cells. But, folks buy their books because they promise results. Here's a newsflash. If God ain't in it, you will never be happy.

Looking for an energy boost that will keep you productively hyper all day long? Buy an energy drink or one of those small quicker-picker-uppers that they sell at the counter of your local Indian Mart. Or you could listen to your body trying to tell you to rest and actually do it. Resting is also mentioned in God's Word a time or two. God and His Word helps you to set priorities in life so that you don't have to work so hard.

But, people continue searching for a better life. Many of us already know that life is better and complete because of Jesus. He fills the gap in our heart like sheet rock mud. He's all we need!

Paul was warning the Colossians to be careful of all those smooth talkin'

philosophers out there. They speak some intelligent words and may seem like they have a cure-all for life, but if God ain't in it, it's a crop of crap! He wanted them to stay rooted, built up and strengthened in Jesus and being thankful for all that He's done.

This would apply to us. We have to study His Word, pray, and realize the Holy Spirit is guiding and teaching us. We should follow Jesus' example in the Bible.

Folks shouldn't go out there seeking God from any other sources like religions, cults and hair-brained philosophies. Seek Jesus! That's where you'll find Him.

Paul goes on in verse 13 to remind the Colossians that before Jesus, they were dead in their sins and sinful nature, but because of Jesus they were made alive. They were forgiven of all of their sins and weren't bound to religious laws and regulations. They weren't bound to evil or to what the world had to offer. Jesus nailed it all to the cross.

If I had to put this into simple terms for us today, it would mean, as Christians, we have freedom. Just like the Colossians, we aren't bound to anything of this world. We don't owe a 'sin debt'. All of our sins are forgiven. Period.

We answer to Jesus and no one has the authority to judge us. They can help us from time to time by offering some cool Christian living tips (as long as its backed by Biblical truths), but other than that, no judging.

Rules for Holy Living
Colossians 3: 1-17

You wanna live a holy life in the world that's pleasing to God?
Here's the 'low down' and the stuff that God doesn't like:

Sexual Immorality
Impurity
Lust
Evil Desires
Greed (Idolatry)

In addition:

Anger
Rage
Malice
Slander
Filthy Language
Lying to each other

Try these on for size. God likes this stuff:

Compassion
Kindness
Humility
Gentleness
Patience
Bear with one another
Forgiveness

And most importantly (covers all):

Love

This is how to achieve holy living. It takes time to get there, but it's worth it. As Christians, our new life in Jesus should reflect God. Just sayin'.

Rules for Christian Households
Colossians 3: 18 – 4: 1

Wanna have a Christian household? This will involve effort from everyone living in our home. Wives, husbands, and the kids will need to work together to make this happen. These tips are simple, but our rebellious attitude makes them hard to follow. But, if we want peace in our homes, this is how we will find it:

Wives
Submit to your husbands.

This information would be enough to make a woman cringe. In today's world, submission means surrender and letting someone with facial hair have complete charge over us. If we are self sufficient, why in the world would we need a ruling authority telling us what to do in a marriage? That just doesn't sound cool.

Let's keep this in mind. God put this information in the

Bible and He invented marriage. This was His plan and He set the whole deal up. He's perfect and knows what He's doing. Right?

So, what would it mean to submit? It would be for the woman to allow the man to be the leader of the home and make the final decisions for the family. This will work if the husband is doing his duties that God has given him. If he is doing his part, then he should be treating his wife as if she were gold and putting her best interest before his own.

Husbands
Love your wives and don't be 'harsh' to them.

Love your wives? Ephesians 5:25 uses the example of Jesus and the church to illustrate how the husband should treat his wife. What did Jesus do for the church? He laid down His life for it. What does this mean?

Fellas, we gotta treat the ladies with respect. We have to really love them. We can't go around treating them like crap. Since Jesus is our leadership example, we need to apply His way of doing things to ours. Know what I'm saying?

We might have to start buying our wives flowers and junk on those special occasions. We might have to take a 6-week training course on 'How To Be

Romantic". And we might even have to sit and watch one of them romantic comedy movies with them and pretend to enjoy it, but that might be taking it a little too far.

The key is to love them. If the ladies are doing their God-given duties, then everything will work out fine.

Kids

Obey your parents in everything.

This is an extremely important rule for kids. It's actually a command from God 'cause it's one of the Ten Commandments zapped on one of them stone tablets Moses was holding. Number 5 to be exact. It's also the first one that comes with a promise. As a kid, you'll live longer for obeying it. That's what the Bible says.

If you look around the world today, you'll see a bunch of wild hooligan kids that seem to have no respect for their parents. This has been going on for quite a while. Even in my childhood, I was part of that unruly bunch. And I bet you were, too.

It seems like society is also helping in the creation of these little monsters by frowning down on parents that 'whoop' their kids. Now I don't think we should go around beating the tar out of them out of anger, but a little butt whoopin' will give them an eye opening consequence for their actions. This needs to happen earlier in their life when their young. That's my two cents.

For the teenagers out there, it's not too late. This will need some Jesus-intervention in the home. Parents will need to become leaders and seek Jesus' guidance for themselves and to pray for their kids. The Lord can work wonders in the home if we allow Him to.

Kids need to realize what the Bible says about this and know the importance of doing what it says. Obey your parents.

To get our home to function according to God's plan will require

a 'come to Jesus' meeting. Group up as a family and talk about it. Know your role and do your job according to what God's Word says. Before long, the family will begin to run smoothly. It's going to take everybody doing their part, keeping God first in everything, and praying about stuff. Working together like a family should.

Paul also mentioned slaves and masters in these verses because it was a common practice in the home back in the day. People had slaves that worked for them. The people were called masters because they had slaves.

That's just how it was back then. Today, this scenario would be considered 'the workplace' or 'our jobs'. Here are some tips from these verses that create a people-friendly atmosphere at 'the workplace':

Slaves (Employees)
Do what your boss tells you to do on the job whether they are watching you or not.

The funny part of this is knowing that there were 'clock milkers' back in those days, too. This is basically folks that work when the boss is around, but as soon as they walk away, they stand around idle waiting for the clock bell to ring saying it's time to go home.

We're all guilty of this, but in order to create a peaceful atmosphere in the workplace according to the Bible, we should do what we are being paid to do. In this current economy, there are hundreds of people that would love to have our jobs. And if we were bosses, who would we choose as an employee? A non-performer? Or someone that's willing to do what we pay them for?

Not doing what the boss tells us to do causes a conflict; arguments happen and feelings get hurt. At worse, our bank accounts get smaller because we're outside holding up 'Will Work For Food' signs. That's when it gets serious.

Whatever you do, work at it with all your heart as if you're doing 'your job' for the Lord.

This is a motivational verse right here. If you're on your job and you're working as if you were serving the Lord with it, it should make you more productive and happier. I know the boss will be smiling. This new mindset will freak them out! They will be so blown away with this new positive attitude and work ethic. It could possibly lead you into better opportunities in the future. Who knows?

Masters (The Boss)
Provide your workers what is right and fair. Remember, you also have a Master, a Boss, in Heaven.

Here's a quick note to the bosses out there. Treat your employees good – pay them fairly and provide them with the correct tools to do the job. Look for ways to help them become more productive and to succeed. Keep in mind, God in Heaven is your Boss. How would you like Him to treat you? Use that example and share the info with your corporate buddies at the next board meeting.

Just think. With a simple Godly mindset change, you could save money from buying those motivational posters that hang up in the employee break room or all of that crappy incentive merchandise that you give them. God's plan works ya'll!

Further Instructions
Colossians 4: 2-6

Paul is telling the folks at Colosse to be praying and to devote some time into it. You know, you can't help but think about our own prayer time after reading a verse like this. How often do you pray?

For me, I have always made it a point to pray every day. Sounds  like a good thing, doesn't it? Unfortunately, I am guilty of doing it as the last thing to do before going to bed. The problem for me is that there is a slight chance of dozing off in the process. You know what I mean? And I've done that before. I'll be praying, and the next thing I know, I'm sawing logs before I say 'amen'. Has this happened to you before?

Devoting time to prayer is important and should be on the daily 'to-do list' like brushing our teeth and taking a morning poo. Even though we pray for the same things every day, that's OK. That's called being persistent in our requests. God's cool with that.

Prayer is a great way of communicating with God. Make it personal. Talk about your day and get things off your chest. That's what He wants us to do. According to this scripture, we should also be watchful and thankful in prayer. This would mean keeping our eyes open for the answer. Expect an answer to happen. It might not be exactly the one you're looking for, but it will be an answer that is best for you. God is good at that kind of stuff. And thank Him ahead of time for it. That's faith right there!

In verse 3 and 4, Paul was requesting prayer for himself and the folks involved in his ministry. He was looking for an 'open door' to share his message. He wanted the folks in Colosse to pray to God for opportunities. He wanted to be able to share it clearly with them, too – in a plain and simple language that they could easily understand. That's pretty cool right there!

That's what we all should be praying for. As folks involved in ministry, we should hope for the 'open door' to tell folks about Jesus and hopefully lead them to Him. Wouldn't that be cool? And our words that lead them should be so simple that even a child could get it. That's what Paul was talking about.

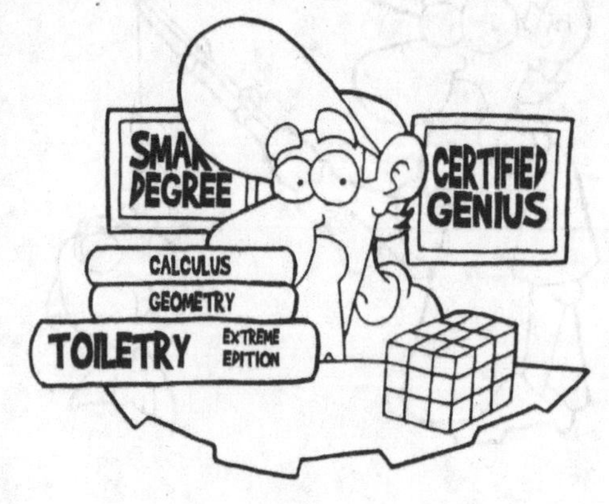

We could use the PhD approach and explain to a lost person the nuclear physical principles of how a cross is made or explain the physio-dynamics of the metallurgical structure of nails, but that junk will fly right over someone's head and they could really care less. People need to know about Jesus and why He died for them. We should explain that to them in simple terms.

As Christians, we need to be wise in the way we act around folks. People are watching. We are representing Jesus out there to a lost and dying world. Our actions and conversations are part of the witnessing tool box that people pay close attention to whether we know it or not. We should choose them wisely.

Final Greetings
Colossians 4: 7-18

These are Paul's final words in this letter to the church in Colosse. It appears that he is sending a couple of folks their way to fill them in on the stuff that's been going on.

Two fellas – Tychicus and Onesimus. Goofy names, but their purpose was to share the ministry's trials and victories with the Colossians. These testimonies would become encouragement for the church and help them to keep pressing on in their ministry as well.

It's important to talk to other believers about the stuff that goes on in our lives. Don't just tell them all of the good things that happen. Tell them about the bad stuff, too. As Christians, we go through some junk from time to time. We need to share that with each other. Not only does it give us an opportunity to pray together about it, it's also encouraging to know that other people are going through the same crap we are. We can then know that we're not alone in our struggles.

If we only shared the 'good stuff' all the time, Christians folks may get discouraged with their own self and wonder why only 'bad things' seem to happen to them. You know what I'm saying? We need to tell the whole story.

Here's an example. Let's say you got a flat tire on your car and got blessed with a new one. Don't go around telling people, "I got a new tire!"

Tell them, "You know, I had a blowout the other day while I was on the expressway. I almost took everyone out driving on the right lane. It was ugly. But I managed to make it to the side of the road, and to my surprise, there was a brand spanking new tire already mounted and balanced on a wheel that matches mine exactly."

This story tells them of the struggle, the stress, and how the Lord helped you through it. That's something they can relate to.

After reading verses 10 through 18, I get the impression that Paul and few of his buddies are sitting chained up in a jail cell somewhere. He's writing a letter to the Colossians and a few of them give a shout out, "Hey! Tell 'em I said hey and junk." There were a few of them; Aristarchus, Mark (Barnabas' cousin), Jesus (whose real name is Justus), Epaphras, Luke (the doctor), and Demas.

The scene in my mind is kinda neat. These interesting fellas are sitting in prison – the end of their rope as ministers – and one of them is writing a letter that is still being read almost 2000 years later. Ain't that cool? Who woulda thunk it?

The lesson here is that if God is using you, you may not see the results right away. Or it could be that the small 'insignificant' thing that you're doing for the Lord may be bigger than what you could imagine. So go ahead and write that song from your heart, write that cool inspirational story, or speak those words that God has given you. Complete that work! Let Him use it for His glory and leave the details to Him.

The Book Of
1st Thessalonians

The Book Of 1ˢᵗ Thessalonians

Introduction To 1ˢᵗ & 2ⁿᵈ Thessalonians

Today we began studying from the Books of Thessalonians (1ˢᵗ & 2ⁿᵈ). I'm sure we've heard this name a time or two. Maybe it was from Sunday School or from a sermon where we had to thumb the pages in our Bible to find it. The cool thing is that there are 2 parts — part I and part II. A sequel? That must mean it has some good stuff in it.

Thessalonians is a letter to the church in Thessalonica written by

the one and only Apostle Paul. He did a lot of writing back in the day. This could be because he spent a lot of his time in prison. I've never been in prison personally, but I hear there's not much to do other than lift weights, read and watch TV. I guess Paul liked to write.

This letter was written around A.D. 51 while Paul was in Corinth. He started this church in Thessalonica and it was young and new. This letter was written only after two or three years since it started. Paul wanted to help strengthen these Christians and to remind them of Jesus' return.

Undoubtedly, there were some confusion about His 'second coming', so Paul wrote this to help them clearly understand.

Let's dig into Thessalonians and see what's in there that we can apply to our own lives. As with all scriptures in the Bible, it's purpose is to help us grow in our faith and spiritual knowledge. I'm sure Thessalonians has something to offer.

Thanksgiving For The Thessalonians' Faith
1 Thessalonians 1: 1-10

The church in Thessalonica seemed to be a good church. Despite their sufferings, they were doing the right things and living right. Actually they were doing such a great job that people around them started to take notice. And to take it another step further, these 'watchers' were talking about it. Paul was excited about this.

This is what 'being a light in the world' is all about right here. As Christians, our life should beam a big beacon of bright halogens to the community around us. Very similar to the

Thessalonians, who were a bunch of idol worshippin' heathens before they met Jesus, our changed lives can shine out to others, too. And folks will start talking about it. That's a good thing!

One of the problems for Christians today is that some choose to live the same lifestyle they had before they were saved. Despite the convictions in their heart about it, they continue this old way of life. It doesn't show a change. Jesus set the example for us to follow and that's what we are supposed to do. Our new life should lead others to Him.

If we stay rooted in the Lord and stay on the right path, the change will follow. This new change will get attention by those around us. People are gonna see it and talk about it. Many of these folks will want it because of the emptiness they feel inside. They may even ask you how they can get some. You see what I'm saying?

Paul's Ministry In Thessalonica
1 Thessalonians 2: 1-16

Paul suffered in sharing the gospel with the Thessalonians when he visited with them the first time. This was back when he helped start the church. He had just been released from prison in Phillipi and was in there for doing the same exact thing – sharing the gospel. You would think he would have learned his lesson? But, apparently not.

He was bold and stood his ground when it came to sharing Jesus with folks, even though a majority of the crowd was against him. Could we be brave enough to do the same? Yeah, God was there to help him, but it didn't keep folks from attacking him. They didn't want to hear what he had to say. What kept him from quitting? It seemed to be a losing game.

Paul knew he was sent on a mission from God to share the Gospel with people. His purpose was to be a vessel (a tool) for God to use to deliver the message. Paul wasn't trying to please people out there. He wasn't in it for money. He wasn't looking for a 'pat on the back' either. This man was 'souled out' for the Lord despite the brick walls he faced. He knew it was for a higher purpose – reaching the lost for Jesus.

This should be our mission, too. We should allow the Lord to use us to reach people. Those gifts and talents we have, that He gave us, is part of the tool box. We need to be about the Lord's business.

Here's the scenario. The world is full of lost people that don't know Jesus as their Lord and Savior. Many of these people cross our paths every day. Yet, we don't share the Gospel with them. Why? Are we afraid of being made fun of? Or have we became so comfy in our own lives that we forget about them and the fact that Jesus is returning soon? Time's running out folks!

We need to love people enough to want to make sure that they are secured in Jesus. We should tell folks our testimony of how He has worked in our lives and not use the Bible like a hammer. Be gentle with them. Paul says, "... like a mother cares for her children." Be encouraging and comforting, "... like a father is with his kids." If we decide to step out for Jesus and be used by Him, we should do it out of love for one another. Ya know?

Paul's Longing To See The Thessalonians

1 Thessalonians 2: 17 – 3: 5

It seems that Paul wanted to visit this church, but wasn't able. The Thessalonians were new Christians and needed some encouragement and guidance in their faith and could've used some help from Paul's teachings. But, it wasn't going to happen. He was hindered. Even though Paul wanted to be

there, it seems that Satan had put up a brick wall. So instead, Paul sent Timothy.

Even though we don't know exactly how Satan prevented Paul from visiting them, we do know that he did. It could've been anything from an illness to hazardous road conditions for his camel. Satan was up to no good. 2 Corinthians 4:4 calls Satan the 'god of this world' in the King James version and 'the god of this age' in the New International version. What does this mean?

This tells me that Satan is in charge of the junk that goes on in this world. He can prevent us from doing the Lord's work. I believe that's why many people get hindered and ministries seem to reach stopping points in their efforts for the Lord. It's like Satan puts out road blocks and speed bumps so that we can't move forward. It's usually at this point where we get discouraged and quit. But, we can't.

God is in charge of everything and is in full control of every situation. He's in control of Satan, too. In the case of Paul, the mission was still accomplished. It wasn't by Paul himself, but through Timothy. God worked it out to have His will be done through someone else despite of the brick wall that Satan built.

It almost sounds like a play in football. The defensive side (Satan) is blocking the offensive side (Paul), while at the same time, the ball gets handed to Timothy to clearly run and score the touchdown (meeting the Thessalonians). That's kinda cool.

This should be an encouragement to anyone that is full-heartedly serving the Lord. Regardless of the obstacles we face, the mission will get accomplished. God is in control and regardless of what seems hopeless, God has a plan. We just have to keep on keepin' on and trust Him.

In the process, we can build our character and perseverance. We can also develop a sensitivity to our brothers and sisters in Christ that are going through some junk in their life.

Verse 19 kinda sums it up for the purpose behind why Paul does what he does. He didn't do all of this cool ministering stuff for the money and fame. We learn that he didn't get rich from it. He didn't do it for the supreme title. It never said that he had an office with his name engraved on a nameplate. A lot of folks didn't like him or even want to hear what he had to say.

Paul did it for the Lord and for the people that would come to know Jesus as their Lord and Savior. This a much bigger reward than you can get here in this world. It's spiritual! Know what I mean?

We should ask ourselves, "What is the true motive behind what we do for the Lord?" If it's for anything other than for Him and leading folks to Him, we might want to get our hearts right.

If our motives are right, then we might not get so mad or discouraged when things don't go our way. Ouch!

Timothy's Encouraging Report
1 Thessalonians 3: 6-13

Timothy returned back to Paul and the gang with some good news. The Thessalonians were doing great! Their faith and love was in check and seemed to have this whole 'being a Christian' thing down pat. Paul was glad to hear it.

This news was encouragement to Paul's ministry team. Keep in mind, Paul and the group were going through some junk for Jesus' sake. They were being spiritually pile driven and body slammed for sharing the Gospel. I'm sure everything was going wrong and then here comes Timothy. If it were me, I would automatically be expecting to hear some more bad news. I would have prepared myself to hear something awful — like maybe the Thessalonians were transformed into a bunch of idol worshipers and had built a big statue of their 'new god' in the sanctuary of their church building. That would've been terrible!

But, nope! It was good news! This would have been a breath of fresh air. In the midst of trouble, this information was encouragement to keep pressing on. I would bet that Paul's strength was restored to keep going.

That's how it is in our Christian walk. Things around us could be rough and it seems like we have become beaten down and spiritually drained. Then out of nowhere, God sends someone to say the right thing at the right time. Or He may allow some 'good news' to come into our life to build us back up again. We should be thankful.

We should also allow God to use us to deliver some 'good news' to one another. One of our coolest jobs as Christians is to be an encouragement to someone. People need to hear it. We need the love of Jesus in our hearts to be able to reach out to them and share this love with encouraging words. We are all in this together and should build each other up. It could be as simple as saying the right things at the right time. Pray the Lord gives you the right things to say to someone in their time of need.

Living to Please God
1 Thessalonians 4: 1-12

Sanctification is the process of living the Christian life. It's not some kind of scientific formula made from 100% natural ingredients that you drink and it cleans you all up inside. It's having the Holy Spirit living inside you; directing and guiding your life to be more like Jesus. The day you accepted Jesus as Lord and Savior and asked for forgiveness of all of your junk, the process began. Living this life is what pleases God. That means He wants us to live this way. He likes that!

The Bible is full of ways to live a sanctified life. Paul gives the church in Thessalonica a few quick helpful tips from these verses that we should take note.

Avoid Sexual Immorality
We should learn to control our bodies in a way that's holy and honorable. Examples of what is sexually immoral is explained throughout the Bible. We live in a world where a lot of it is made acceptable, but not in God's eyes. Read up on it and know for yourself. Here's a few:

Adultery (Exodus 20:14)
Fornication (Hebrews 13:4)
Sexual Perversions (Leviticus 18:6, 22-24)
Sex on the Brain (Matthew 5:28)

Love Each Other
Plain and simple. This doesn't mean to just love the folks that are close to us like family and friends. This means to love everybody – including the fella that cut you off on the expressway.

Lead A Quiet Life

People don't need to know your business and you shouldn't go around stirring up drama. The perfect place to do all of this these days seems to be on social networking sites like Facebook. Amen? If you want to hear the 'low down' in someone's life, sign up by creating a page and add them as a friend. And let the drama begin. The Lord wants us to live a quiet life, which means we don't have to share everything that goes on in our life as 'status updates'.

Mind Our Own Business

This would mean not adding our 'two cents' to someone else's drama and staying out of their affairs. Know what I'm saying? There's a difference in helping someone with their problems and just flat-out being nosy in someone's life. Know the difference.

Work With Our Hands

We should all be willing to work. If the Lord opens a door for us to work, then we should do it. We should go to those jobs that He has given us and actually do something while we're there. I mean, that's what we are being paid to do. Right?

What it boils down to is gaining the respect from others. By simply following these tidbits of information, people will learn to respect us for who we are by what we do and not do. It's not so that we can look 'all good and all' in their eyes, but our life will reflect Jesus. People will most likely hear the Good News Of Jesus from someone they can respect. You see?

The Coming of the Lord
1 Thessalonians 4: 13 - 5: 11

In case you haven't heard the news. Jesus is coming back!

This may come as a shock to some of you, but this is the big day that many of us Christians have been waiting for. It's going to be an awesome time because it means that we will be leaving all of our worries and troubles behind. It means that we are going to see our loved ones again that have passed on in death. It's also going to be the first time we have seen Jesus face-to-face.

All of the skeptics and

303

doubters will stand in surprise because now they can see for themselves what all those crazy Christian people have tried to warn them about. Now it's gonna be too late!

So, how's it all going to go down? According to these scriptures, it says at first:

1) There will be a loud command
2) There will be a voice of the archangel
3) There will be a trumpet call from God
4) Jesus will come down from Heaven

Around about the same time:

1) The dead in Christ shall rise.
   a) This is kinda creepy because that would mean that graves of Christians would bust wide open.

2) Christians, that are still alive when Jesus comes, will join the dead in the clouds to meet Him in the air.
   a) This means folks are going to be airborne – no parachute needed.

You see how dramatic this is going be? This is the day that we, as Christians, have been waiting for. That's why it's so important for us to share the news.

So, you're probably thinking, "That sounds all cool and all, but does the Bible say when it's going to happen? 'cause if I knew the exact date, I could get my life together maybe a day before the event. This will allow me to 'live it up' until then. Ya know?"

The answer is 'no'. Actually it plainly states that Jesus will come like a thief in the night. It will be a date that no one knows. It could be during a time of worldly peace when everything in life flows like butter. Who knows?

The key is to be ready. As Christians, we need to make sure we are living right so that we are able to lead others to Jesus. We should work together as brothers and sisters in Christ by encouraging and strengthening one another. This is a serious deal!

Final Instructions
1 Thessalonians 5: 12-28

Paul ends this letter to the Thessalonians with what seems to be a long list of To-Do's and Don'ts. He undoubtedly considers this list important because he tells us that this is God's will for us. These are probably pertaining to the church setting. Let's look at them:

Respect those that work hard, who are over you in the Lord?
- This could mean

respecting the folks in charge of the church that we attend. This would be the elders, deacons, etc. These folks do a lot for the church and should be shown some respect for it.

Live in peace with each other?

- Don't be a troublemaker or stir up junk. We should do what we can to maintain the peace.

Warn those that are idle?

- In the church, everybody has a job to do. There's always something that can be done. Being lazy ain't cool and hinders the body of Christ. If you need a job to do in the church, you can always ask your church secretary. They're usually up to speed on what needs to be done.

Encourage the timid?

- Another word for 'timid' is 'shy'. Sometimes folks stand around in the church not helping simply because they are too shy to ask. Spot them and help them get acquainted with the church and its people. Find them something to do.

Help the weak?

- This could mean the folks in the church

that are not as scripturally knowledgeable of the Bible as you are. It could be our fellow brothers and sisters in Christ who have become weak in their faith. We gotta help those people.

Be patient with everybody?

- Count to ten when you feel like you're going to freak out on some of the church folks. When your on your last nerve, take a breather. Be patient.

Make sure nobody pays wrong for wrong?

- This never solves problems. It only creates a bigger flame in the fire. Do what's right according to what God's Word says. Learning to turn the other cheek could help in this situation.

Always be kind to everybody?

- Yep, it says everybody. There are a variety of people that visit churches on any given week. The last thing they want to hear is something negative from a rude church person. That's the perfect excuse for them not to come back. Plus, we should also be kind to the folks we fellowship with every week. It creates a happy place that folks will love to come to.

Be joyful always?

- Be happy! There's so much to smile about. If you're saved today, you should be showing teeth. Ain't that enough to bring you joy? Folks need to see it. Especially in the rural area that your church sets in.

Pray continually?

- Prayer is the way we communicate with God. Keep those lines open and do it often. As a church, we should stay in-tune with the Lord and we do this through prayer. To be effective in the community, we need His guidance to do His will. Prayer helps us realize what it is.

Give thanks in all circumstances?

- Has the Lord done something for you recently? Give Him thanks. Even if He hasn't, we should be thankful to Him anyway. I'm sure we'll discover something to be thankful for. It might not necessarily be in material things, but having air to breathe is vital for life. Thank Him for that.

Do not put out the Spirit's fire?

- When the Holy Spirit is working in a person or in a church, you are going to see some fruit and some changed lives. If you don't see 'fire' happening around you, it may be smothered with some sinful junk. Poke at it with God's Word. Get that fire going again.

Do not treat prophecies with contempt?

- A prophecy is a God-inspired message. It is of the most importance delivered by someone to share with folks that need to hear it. We can't just ignore it or laugh it off. We should compare it to God's Word and apply it if the message is to us.

Test everything?

- Just because a preacher says it, doesn't make it true. Test everything that appears to be right with God's Word. That way you'll know for sure.

Hold on to the good?

- Always remember the good things the Lord has done. This will help you keep the faith when the troubles come.

Avoid every kind of evil?
- The best way to prevent sin from happening is to avoid the temptation. Turn away from it. Don't allow it around you. For the church, don't sugar coat God's Word for the sake of evil. If the Bible says something is wrong, don't allow it in the church.

According to Paul, this was God's will for the church. We are all being sanctified by simply living the Christian life. Our ultimate goal is to live like Jesus.

The Book Of
2nd Thessalonians

The Book Of 2ⁿᵈ Thessalonians

Thanksgiving and Prayer
2 Thessalonians 1: 1-12

Paul was proud of the church in Thessalonica. Their faith was growing stronger and the love they had for one another was increasing. They stood their ground when facing trials and persecutions. They endured! Wow! According to Paul, they would be considered worthy of the kingdom of God.

How would we measure up? Are we doing everything we're supposed to do as Christians? I know our answer would be something like:

"No one's perfect! So, I'm wingin' it!"

"I'm sorta hangin' in there and doing what I can to get by."

Think about this. How's our faith in Jesus? Are we stronger than we were the day we accepted Him as Lord and Savior? It should be. If not,

what is it in your life that's stopping you from growing spiritually?

And what about love? Do you find yourself loving people more and more? If not, why not?

Here's another one. How well do you stand the trials and junk that comes into your life? Do you buckle under pressure? If so, why aren't you trusting in the Lord?

These are things that Paul was complimenting the Thessalonians about. They would be counted worthy because they have stood the tests.

God's judgment is coming when He returns for both the good and bad. For Christians, we have to make sure we are giving Him our best until He gets here. We all have a purpose and we should be fulfilling it. We have to endure! We have to do what the Lord tells us to do. Endure!

The Man of Lawlessness
2 Thessalonians 2: 1-12

Based on these verses, I can only assume that someone sent a counterfeit letter to the church in Thessalonica and signed it with Paul's name. The letter stated that the Lord had already came back the second time. It could have been presented through some false teaching. Who knows? All they knew was that all hope was gone. Can you imagine the doom and gloom that was going on? How would you feel if you thought you missed the Glorybound Train to Eternity? That would sorta stink!

I am glad Paul sent this letter. And I bet they were, too. It cleared up some confusion about Jesus' return. These verses can share some light into our lives about it as well.

Even in today's world, people have been predicting this glorious return for hundreds of years. We call it 'The End of the World". As a matter of fact, we got one coming up in December of 2012. This expiration date was predicted by the Mayans or on the fact that their calendar will run out of dates. Ooh! I can't wait! People are going to be going nuts.

315

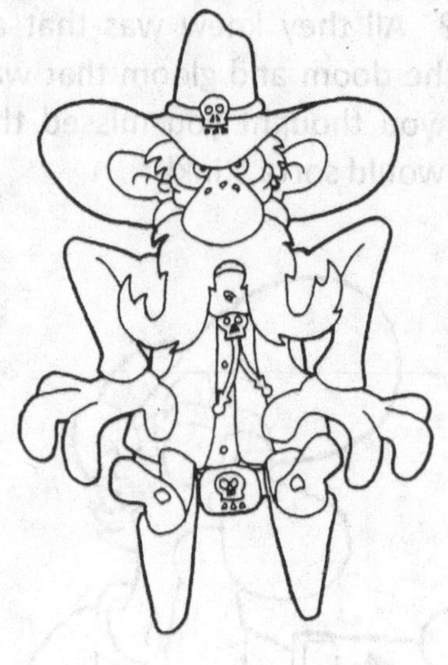

Paul told the Thessalonians that something spectacular had to happen first. He mentions the 'man of lawlessness". Sounds like a cowboy western movie, don't it? Paul tells them that a rebellion has to occur and the man of lawlessness is revealed. This person flops himself on the scene and exalts himself over everything God-related and even proclaims to be God. He will 'setup shop' in God's temple and will probably expect folks to worship him. He will be working with the power of Satan and will be able to do some cool tricks – miracles, signs, and wonders – that will amaze people. I'm sure there will be a crowd following him and he might even have his own website and Twitter. He will be the anti-Christ.

For years, we have been trying to figure out the 'mystery' of who the anti-Christ is. In my lifetime, I think we've pinned the name on every President that's been elected into office. We have also thought maybe some of the foreign leaders with

the funny sounding names

could've been the one or possibly a couple of the corporate big-money business owners. Maybe some of the high-follutin' religious celebrities. But, the fact is that we really don't know. Whoever it is, this person is going to be powerful and lead a lot of folks the wrong way.

As Christians, we have to stay rooted in Jesus and keep the faith. It probably wouldn't be a good idea to broadcast our thoughts on who we think the 'anti-Christ' is because we're going to look like some kinda 'religious weirdo' to the folks we're trying to lead to the Lord.

And another thing. We don't have to be afraid of this 'anti-Christ' fella because he has already been defeated. We know how the story is going to end. God is in control! We need to be prepared for Jesus' return and to continue sharing the Gospel to the folks that need to hear it.

Stand Firm
2 Thessalonians 2: 13-17

If you're saved today, you're in good shape. You are part of God's family. When Jesus returns, you are out of here. Gone! Hear me?

Here again, we have to stay rooted in Jesus while we're here on Earth. Hold on to the teachings from the Bible. We need to live our lives the way Jesus lived His. He is our example, folks! This process is called sanctification because we are allowing the Holy Spirit to help us grow as Christians to be more like Jesus.

Our job here is to tell others how to receive salvation. This is called The Great Commission and every one of us has this responsibility. The reason Paul is telling the church in Thessalonica to 'stand firm' is because he knows it's not a smooth sailing boat ride. The same applies to us. We are going to face some tidal waves – false teachings, persecutions, trials, and worldly temptations. Stand firm!

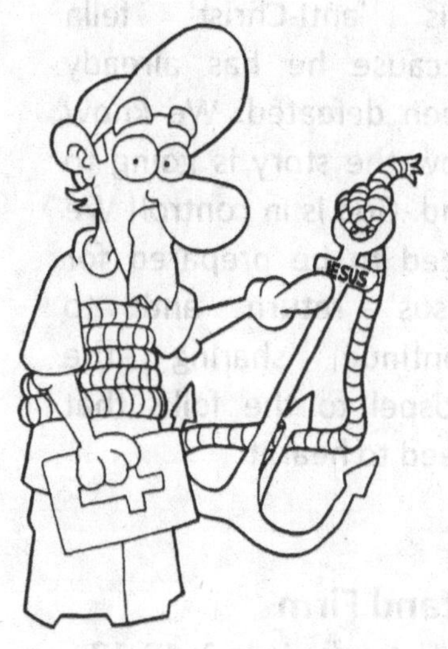

We have to hold on tight to God's Word – the stuff from the Bible. Cling to Jesus. His anchor holds!

Request for Prayer

2 Thessalonians 3: 1-5

Paul is requesting prayer from the Thessalonians that his ministry continued to share the message of the Lord. He wanted it to spread rapidly and for the folks to receive it in their hearts. I take it he wasn't a 'feel good' preacher that only told people what they wanted to hear and made them feel all gooey inside. He was leading folks to Jesus and delivered a message that exposed sin and gave them a remedy for it... Jesus.

Paul requested they pray for their protection from the 'evil and wicked' folks that personally didn't want to hear a word of what they had to say. He knew he was up against some serious obstacles and dangerous ground. It wasn't a hike through a flower garden. They could've been killed. Seriously!

In America, it may not be so dangerous sharing God's Word with people. The worst obstacle we may face is having someone laugh at us. But in other countries, you can be killed for it. That's why we should pray for our missionaries that go out in the world. Some of them go where 'no man has gone before'. And there's a reason why people don't go there. It's called 'flying bullets and Christians are the target'. Yeah, I know... they need prayer!

From these verses, we also realize that spiritual attacks are real and are to be expected. As Christians, we are going to face them. We should pray for strength and help from God, study His Word so that we will know what to do when we are being attacked and use the promises in there to fight against them. Tough it out because God is on our side.

Warning Against Idleness
2 Thessalonians 3: 6-15

Paul was telling the Thessalonians to stay away from the 'lazy' folks and to follow his example instead. He wanted them to stay busy and work.

These folks were wrongly believing that Jesus was returning very soon – like probably in the next few days or something. Because of this, they stopped doing anything. They wouldn't work and weren't productive in their lives. They depended on the church for financial support. Instead of being busy with working, they became 'busybodies' and spent their time gossiping. That's not good.

"If a man won't work, he won't eat." That was the rule Paul gave when he was with them. In verses 14 and 15, he was basically telling the church to cut them off financially. If these folks started starving, maybe they would get up and finally do something about it... like 'work' and junk.

In this situation, there were jobs available and things that needed to be done. Some of these people chose to not do anything but wait for the Lord to return. Paul was motivating them to do something.

In this current economic situation in the world today, there are a lot of folks not working. It wasn't by choice. It's just how the cookie crumbled. For Christians out there unemployed, God promises to take care of them.

But my God shall supply all your need according to his riches in glory by Christ Jesus. - Philippians 4: 19

A situation like this is different than what is explained from the scriptures in Thessalonians. Those people had an opportunity to work and chose not to. I believe if God opens a door for us to work, then we should. If there's not an open door, then we have to keep trusting God to take care of us and wait for the open door. We can use this available time to serve Him in whatever capacity He gives us.

The worst thing we can do is become busybodies. If we have time to sit around talking about people and stirring up trouble, we have time to use it more productively to work and serve the Lord.

Final Greetings
2 Thessalonians 3: 16-18

Paul ends this letter with words of peace. He also assures them that this was really his letter written with his own hand.

The sad thing to me is knowing that he even had to say that. But, you know, false teachers back in the day were writing their own letters to the churches providing their own ideas of how it should be run. Many of them would forge Paul's signature at the end so that the church would feel confident in reading it and actually do what it says.

This should be an eye opener to us that 'false teaching' has been going on for a long time. If it was popular in A.D. 52, I can only imagine how much more false teaching is going on in the world today. We have to really be careful of what we are being taught. Ya know?

Just because a person wears a suit and has a theological degree, it doesn't make him or her the real deal. That certificate on their wall doesn't make them certified to share God's Word. We are going to have to educate ourselves and study God's Word on our own and shouldn't rely on someone to do it for us. When preachers preach, we should compare what they say with what the Bible says. And when religions start whipping out these booklets that they say are Bible additions, you might as well walk away. The Bible is complete!

It's a tricky world out there, so be careful. Satan is in full motion to deceive us. We have to put on the full armor of God mentioned in Ephesians 6: 10-18:

"Finally, my brethren, be strong in the Lord, and in the power of his might. Put on the whole armour of God, that ye may be able to stand against the wiles of the devil. For we wrestle not against flesh and blood, but against principalities, against powers, against the rulers of the darkness of this world, against spiritual wickedness in high [places]. Wherefore take unto you the whole armour of God, that ye may be able to withstand in the evil day, and having done all, to stand. Stand therefore, having your loins girt about with truth, and having on the breastplate of righteousness; And your feet shod with the preparation of the gospel of peace; Above all, taking the shield of faith, wherewith ye shall be able to quench all the fiery darts of the wicked. And take the helmet of salvation, and the sword of the Spirit, which is the word of God: Praying always with all prayer and supplication in the Spirit, and watching thereunto with all perseverance and supplication for all saints;"

So, gear up! And like Paul said, "The grace of the Lord be with us all."

The Book Of
1ˢᵗ Timothy

The Book Of 1ˢᵗ Timothy

Introduction To 1ˢᵗ & 2ⁿᵈ Timothy - Who is Timothy?

We've heard this name a few times, haven't we? Timothy was a young Christian fella from the Bible. From what I've read, his mother and grandmother led him to the Lord. He looked up to the Apostle Paul and Paul considered him 'his son in the faith'. I would imagine that Timothy learned a lot from him. The both of them went out on missionary journeys together and probably shared the same can of Spam when times were tough. They were a team.

I get the feeling that Paul was like Timothy's teacher because he shared his knowledge with him. This would eventually help him to become a leader. According to the scriptures, Timothy was asked to go to Ephesus alone to help 'square up' the church because of all of the false teaching they were receiving. This was the job of a leader, and for Timothy, it could have been as a Pastor position.

1ˢᵗ and 2ⁿᵈ Timothy (also Titus) are considered Pastoral Letters and offers guidelines on how to run a church more smoothly. The first two are also letters to Timothy to offer him encouragement and instructions as he takes on the job of Gettin' 'er Done!

According to the footnotes of most study Bibles, it says that 1st Timothy was written by Paul back around A.D. 64. His sequel, 2nd Timothy, was written around A.D. 66 or 67. Not really sure, but the dates I'm sure are pretty close.

Timothy, a young Christian leader doing the Lord's work, needed some encouragement. Paul felt the need to send him these letters to boost him up; to get him all fired up. And Paul was someone he could trust. We could learn a thing or two from this. You reckon'?

Warning Against False Teachers of the Law
1 Timothy 1: 1-11

Timothy was instructed by Paul to stay in Ephesus. It seems the church down there was having some problems that needed some special attention. Teachers were spreading a bunch of junk through their religious curriculum instead of sound doctrine. The church in Ephesus was believing it!

According to Paul, these teachers were teaching:

False doctrine
Myths and fables
Endless genealogy
Mumbo jumbo

The problem is that it created a lot of controversy. A good bit of time was being wasted because it was focused on this stuff instead of what the Gospel was all about. Folks weren't doing God's work because they were too busy flim-floppin' with fables and genealogy that didn't matter. Folks were believing this information being taught and began turning away from the truth. Not good!

It also sounds like to me that these teachers were presenting the law and using it for the wrong purposes. It could've been used to make the people feel guilty and to pay a 'love offering' for their bad behavior.

331

Here's the deal. The simple Gospel is that we're all naturally born sinners (lawbreakers). God sent His Son to take the punishment for our sins. He offers us the gift of eternal life. By accepting Jesus as our Lord and Savior would mean to ask Him for forgiveness and for Him to step in to our hearts. That's what being saved is all about. We're saved from sin because of Jesus. You with me?

This same simple Gospel is what we are to share with others. We have to let them know. We can't waste time on religious 'hooplah' that's not important. We have to read the Bible for ourselves to protect ourselves from receiving some bad information. Compare everything you hear with what it says in the Bible. Don't just take someone's word for it.

Timothy had a big job ahead of him. He had to fix this problem in Ephesus. He was young, but Paul saw something

inside of him that let him know that he could handle it.

The Lord's Grace To Paul
1 Timothy 1: 12-20

Paul had a lot to be thankful for. He realized where he had came from and he knew where the Lord brought him. One thing we know about Paul's past was that he was a violent person that hated Christians. Actually he hated them so much, he killed them literally. But, a special event on Damascus Road changed his life forever. Jesus turned his life around and pointed him in the right direction.

Because of this change, Paul was thankful for God's mercy and love for him. Did Paul deserve such awesome treatment? He was a bad man! He shoulda been electrocuted in an electric chair for his crimes, but fortunately electricity wasn't invented yet. But, this change does show a characteristic of God. No matter how bad (or sinful) a person is, God can save them. He loves us all. Isn't that cool?

And to make it extra neat, God can use your terrible past to reach people that are going through the same thing. Your past becomes a testimony of God's grace that will lead them to Him.

We serve a a patient, loving God that has mercy on the world. If you look around you and see all of the stuff that's happening that goes against God, it makes you wonder why He doesn't squish sinful people like water bugs. Love, patience, and mercy! One day people will see their sinful nature and turn to Him before it's too late.

Paul's instruction to Timothy was to encourage him to fight the good fight by keeping the faith with a good conscience. It seems many of the others had gone astray and left their faith behind. What would cause someone to turn their backs on Jesus? Temptation? Sin? Love for money?

The key is to keep your faith in Christ as a number 1 priority in life above everything else. Listen to the Holy Spirit's guidance as

He works through your conscience to help you do what is right at all times. If you know something is wrong or bad for you, don't do it. Listen.

Instructions on Worship
1 Timothy 2: 1-15

These verses were some instructions for the church. Paul starts it out by saying that the church should be a 'praying church' and to include everyone in their prayer requests. This includes the folks in leadership like kings, rulers, and presidents.

I know, in America, we poke fun at our people in authority. With every person in power, you can almost guarantee that there will be a joke to follow. But God wants us to live peaceful and quiet Christian lives. Instead of being the ones making jokes about our President, we should be the ones that are praying for them and lifting them up. This separates us from the world and God likes it.

Verse 9 is where it gets tricky. It seems Paul is doing a little bit of female bashing and expects women to dress all junky at church and to not say a word. Sounds like women shouldn't do their hair all up and to leave their fancy smancy jewelry at home. And when it comes to a woman teaching or having any authority over a man in church, it sounds like a definite no. What's going on here?

I believe Satan can take a few verses from the Bible and convince folks that they mean something that it doesn't. With verses like this, you have to go back in time to when they were written. Why would Paul say this to the church back around A.D. 64? Especially when it's in the Bible of how he was ministered and taught to by a woman. Actually there are several times mentioned where women were a big part of the church. Here's a few:

Women pray! - 1 Corinthians 11:5
But every woman that prayeth or prophesieth with her head uncovered dishonoureth her head: for that is even all one as if she were shaven.

Women teach! - Acts 18: 24-26
And a certain Jew named Apollos, born at Alexandria, an eloquent man, and mighty in the scriptures, came to Ephesus. This man was instructed in the way of the Lord; and being fervent in the spirit, he spake and taught diligently the things of the Lord, knowing only the baptism of John. And he began to speak boldly in the synagogue: whom when Aquila and Priscilla had heard, they took him unto them, and expounded unto him the way of God more perfectly.

Women have church leadership positions! - Romans 16: 1, 2
I commend unto you Phebe our sister, which is a servant of the church which is at Cenchrea: That ye receive her in the Lord, as becometh saints, and that ye assist her in whatsoever business she hath need of you: for she hath been a succourer of many, and of myself also.

Note: A succourer is a person that helps someone in serious times of need. This was a position in the church at Cenchrea and today would be considered an Outreach Ministry or Benevolence Committee – that helped people with hunger, clothing and shelter. An awesome job! Phebe was in charge of it!

Women labor for the church! - Romans 16: 6, 12
Greet Mary, who bestowed much labour on us.

Salute Tryphena and Tryphosa, who labour in the Lord. Salute the beloved Persis, which laboured much in the Lord.

Knowing all of this already, Paul must have had other reasons for not wanting the women in Ephesus talking or doing anything. You think?

You don't reckon it was because the women weren't educated enough to be sharing their thoughts with others? Because in the early Jewish culture, women weren't allowed to study. Plus, since false teaching was running crazy in the churches of that day, uneducated women teaching would've been even more confusing.

Why did he want them to dress modest? And what did he consider 'modest' anyway? According to the verses, he didn't want the ladies to fluff up their hair with fancy hairdos or wear expensive clothes made by Prada, Versace, or Gloria Camelbilt. It would've been a distraction in the church like it is today. Think about how many times you've looked at what folks were wearing that come into your church. Their clothing and appearance determines their financial status. The next thing you know, your mind is set on money instead of what the preacher is saying.

Or it could be that we dress all fancy and junk so that we can get the attention of others. You see where I'm going with this? If everybody dressed simple, no one would be judging each other and distracting ourselves and others in church.

Paul did a little leadership comparison between Adam and Eve. Not that Adam is any better than Eve, but he was explaining why the woman should learn and study for themselves before teaching to a congregation.

According to Genesis 2: 16, 17:

And the LORD God commanded the man, saying, Of every tree of the garden thou mayest freely eat: But of the tree of the knowledge of good and evil, thou shalt not eat of it: for in the day that thou eatest thereof thou shalt surely die.

This was God's command to Adam (not Adam and Eve) because she wasn't invented yet. Adam must've taught this to her later. She received secondhand info and was later tempted by Satan and then sinned.

Paul's purpose of sharing this was probably to let the women know they had the freedom to learn and study. During the time of his writing, the ladies were being neglected and should've been taught God's Word. But until then, it would be best that they remained silent because they would've distracted the church folks with all them questions they had.

Did that make sense?

Overseers and Deacons
1 Timothy 3: 1-16

What is a bishop? The NIV calls it an overseer. What is that position in a church? According to what I have read, it is a church leader. It could be a pastor or a church elder. Paul says that this is a big job with big responsibilities and requires some big demands. Here's a breakdown of the credentials of a church leader:

He must be blameless
A person must have a current clean record so that no one can point fingers. It's kinda hard to listen to a preacher who is currently running a drug business in the community. It just doesn't work! However, if a drug dealer comes to the Lord and ask for forgiveness, his record is cleaned. He can then be able to preach because Jesus pardoned his sin – he is now blameless.

Have 1 wife
Back in the day, men had several wives. To be a church leader, you should only have one. I don't believe a divorced man that wants to become a preacher that has a new wife is subject to this because he is still a man with one wife. Some churches today will not let a divorced man preach because of their false

understanding of this requirement.

Vigilant (temperate)

Sober (self-controlled)

Good behavior (respectable)

Hospitable (be nice to folks)

Be able to teach

Not given to wine (not a drunkard)
Drunk preachers and leaders sound sorta funny. It's hard to take them seriously. It's a good idea to not drink at all if you're in a church leadership position.

Not a striker (not violent but gentle)
No one wants a preacher that is known in the community for kicking butts and starting trouble. It just doesn't look good on the resume. Plus, the folks doing the hiring knows that somewhere down the line that the preacher will be verbally attacked by someone from the congregation. Can you imagine a preacher carrying the Bible in one hand and a machine gun in the other? Not a good combination.

Not greedy of filthy lucre (not a lover of money)
Preachers that love money will probably do what they can to get it. This could mean changing up the sermon to make folks feel guilty so that they will dump their wallets into the offering plate. This could involve some sweet fluffy music playing in the background with a video of starving children from around the world showing in the mix, and then there's the preacher's puppy dog eyes staring at you saying softly, "Won't you give today?"

Patient

Not a brawler

Not covetous

One that rules well with his own house (kids in subjection – his kids will respect him)
I don't think this means that a qualified preacher will have the perfect kids. Actually, one of Satan's weapons used against a man of God is to attack his children. If he can't get the preacher to stumble, he'll work on the kids to make him look bad. However, a preacher's kids will respect him because of how he treats his kids. He will love them and discipline them when needed. Because of this kind of leadership in the home, his kids will

respect him no matter how bad they themselves act outside of the home.

Not a novice (not new to Christianity)
Being a Christian is a growing experience. To be a church leader, you can't expect to lead a church if you yourself haven't even got your feet wet yet. God prepares His people for positions like this and wouldn't just throw you out there inexperienced. You'll go through some training first.

He must have a good report (a good reputation)

A church is judged by it's people and it's leader. Some folks have learned to overlook a few hypocrites in a church, but they will not tolerate a preacher with a bad reputation. If you're preacher is making the Arrest Log in your local paper every week, that's your sign to get him out of your church. He's making it stink! It won't be effective in sharing Jesus in your community.

There are also qualifications to being a Deacon in a church, according to Paul. Falling asleep and snoring in front of the congregation on Sunday morning didn't make the list, But, here's what did:

Must be grave (worthy of respect)

Not double-tongued (sincere)

Not given to much wine (not a drunkard)
It probably wouldn't be a great idea to hold your Deacon Board meeting at the local bar boozing it up while throwing darts and flirting with the waitresses. That's just my opinion.

Not greedy of filthy lucre (not pursuing dishonest gain)
Being a Deacon is about serving others, especially those in the church. Many have used it for financial gain. Check your motives. Would you become a Deacon if it meant cleaning the toilets? Some have this responsibility.

Holding the mystery of the faith in pure conscience

Proved (they must be tested)

Blameless (no records against them)

Husband of one wife

Rules his house and his children respect him

Their wives must be grave, not slanderers, and faithful in all things (the women must be worthy of respect, not backstabbers, temperate and trustworthy.
Not only does the job of a Deacon require certain qualifications from him, but it involves his wife, too. Based on scripture, if a man is married to a trouble-making, back stabbing, loud-mouthin', naggin' woman, he could automatically be disqualified from the job. It wouldn't be based on his credentials, but his wife's. I imagine a woman like this would make him look bad as a leader in the church. I can see why. Can't you?

Instructions to Timothy
1 Timothy 4: 1-16

Paul mentions to Timothy that in the 'latter times' folks are gonna depart (or abandon) the faith and follow the deceptive lies of false teachings. Latter times would, of course, mean later on down the road after the date that Paul wrote this letter. Actually, I believe it's been an ongoing process since that time. It's been a work craftfully performed by demonic forces.

Paul gives a few examples of some of these deceptions like certain meats forbidden to eat and religions where people are forbidden to marry. Today, there are religions out there that actually forbid their followers from doing them:

Food
<u>Buddhism</u> – forbid eating beef products.
<u>Hinduism</u> – avoid pork, fowl, ducks, snails, crabs, and camels. The cow is forbidden.
<u>Islam</u> – forbid eating pork and birds of prey.
<u>Judaism</u> – forbid eating pigs, rabbits and creatures of the sea (such as lobster, shrimp, and clams).
<u>Rastafarianism</u> – forbid eating meat and fish.
Marriage
<u>Catholics</u> – forbid their priests to marry.

I'm sure there are others out there. These are the only ones that I have read about. But, the key here from these verses is that, if God made it, it's good. These are God's gifts to us. We just need to thank Him for it.

These verses tells us that we should train ourselves to be godly. Work at it! Put into practice the life you read about from God's Word. Follow Jesus' example. The benefits from it go beyond a worldly view. It's a spiritual thing.

It's similar to training physically where you get all

pumped up with muscles from lifting weights or running on a treadmill. Over time you might even be able to lift your own weight or be strong enough to run in a marathon. Spiritual 'godly' workouts prepare you for life (good and bad) and help you influence others. It prepares you for the eternal life after this one has gone.

Timothy was a young fella. He was sharing the Gospel with folks including the older folks, too. I'm sure he was up against some grumpy old poots that thought he had no business teaching them nothing. You can't teach an old dog new tricks, right? But, Paul was encouraging him to keep on keepin' on despite of all of the obstacles. He was told to set an example in speech, in life, in love, in faith and in purity. He had a gift and he needed to use it for Jesus.

This applies to us. Believe it or not, we influence people around us. In some cases, our presentation leaves a bad example. Think about our homes. What type of examples are we teaching our kids? How are we affecting our spouses?

What about our jobs? Those people we work with are affected by our actions. It's all about setting examples. Our life should reflect Jesus everywhere we go. People are watching all aspects of our life and taking notes. Just make sure the life you present matches the life that Jesus gave you to follow.

Advice About Widows, Elders and Slaves
1 Timothy 5: 1-25 and 6: 1,2

Paul was giving some advice to Timothy on how to treat people in the church. Since Timothy was a young fella, his approach needed be different to each of the people he would speak to.

Let's say you're a an older fella (maybe in your 50's). You've been to the school of Hard Knocks and learned things that's made you the person that you are. Would you want some young whooper-snapper that's fresh out of the water telling you that you've been doing things all wrong? Of course not!

If you were a young gal in her early 20's, would you want someone your own age telling you serious stuff as if he was your Daddy? Definitely not!

The thing about sharing the Gospel with people is that you have to address them on their level. People want respect and not to be looked down on. We have to think about how they would want to hear it because the way we present it matters. That's what Paul was saying.

Here we have a typical church. People looked to this church for spiritual nourishment, strength, and help when they needed it. If they couldn't turn to their families in times of need, they could always turn to the church. The problem is when everybody is knocking on the church door for a handout. Over time, a church will go broke and people that really need help won't get it because there won't be anything left to help them with. Knowing who to help took a little research.

For example:
Scenario: A widow (a woman who's husband dies) knocks on the church door needing help.

(The church whips out the Widows Needing Help Questionnaire Form)

Disclaimer: To qualify for the church 'Widow Needing Help' program, the widow applicant must be at least 60 years old and meet certain moral and spiritual standards. She must also have a dead husband. Young widows need not apply.

1. Does the widow really need help?
   a. No. Send her on her way.
   b. Yes. <ask the next question>
2. Does the widow have family?
   a. No. The church should help.
   b. Yes. The widow's family should help her. It's Biblical and God likes it when families help each other.

A system like this will work and will benefit a lot of folks in need. Churches today should follow this, too. Many would be more effective in the community if they researched the people they helped and put more of the responsibility of helping them with their own families. And families should work together in love to help one another.

Another item on the church agenda is about the church leaders. Church leaders should be paid wages, especially those that preach and teach. Plus, any accusation against these leaders should be backed up with two or three witnesses.

Our church leaders use a lot of valuable time to do their church duties and should be paid for it. It's OK to pay them and it's OK to accept wages for your services. It's Biblical! These leaders are in front of those pews and work behind the scenes to present that beautiful church service you go to every week. They are also in the church eyes. They are going to be criticized and watched closely, but before we accept any claims against them, we need to hear the proof.

Next item, sin in the church. These verses say call them out publicly. Make it known to the church. Call them by name. This will be as an example to the others. I know that sounds rude and crude, but sin in a church can totally mess up it's effectiveness in the community.

Favoritism? I imagine churches back in the day would select certain 'chosen' people to help. Maybe their friends and families could advance in line on the Help List. This type of stuff still goes on in the church today. You have people that handle the daily business of the church. Because of their high position, their families and friends will get special privileges. That's just how it goes

and it's not right. Plus, some churches give special treatment to it's members that give financial offerings. Here again, this ain't right either. As a church, we can't show favoritism. Do what's right.

Laying hands suddenly on no man? In some religions or Christian practices, laying of hands is being used as a way of praying for someone or to jolt them with some kind of spiritual magic that will rid them of whatever ails them. The purpose for it in these verses meant 'making a decision'. In this case, Paul was telling the church not to make any sudden decisions in selecting their church leaders. This would require God's guidance and prayer. Do your homework and check their credentials.

Sin sharing? As church members and part of God's family, we need to live a life that's pure. We can't go around getting involved in sinful junk during the week and pretend to be saints when we go to church. That's called a hypocrite! People are watching us and we need to be representing Jesus everywhere we go.

Stop drinking only water? Drink a little wine. This sounds like Paul is encouraging Timothy to booze it up from small 6-ounce bottles. But, it's not. Paul was worried about Timothy's health. It could have been that their water had cooties in it and it was messing his stomach up. It's kinda hard to stand and share the Gospel when you're constantly back and forth to the toilet. Paul said drink a 'little' wine. Not grape juice or wine coolers in small bottles. He said wine because it has healthy properties to it and would help ease his stomach. This is not our scripture that makes it OK to become alcoholics and 'winos'. It was used as a medicine.

Slaves should respect their masters? Plain and simple. In today's world, this would be the same as 'workers respecting their bosses'. Paul was telling Timothy that, just because a 'boss' was a Christian, a Christian worker should treat him respectfully as a boss even though he was also a Christian brother in Christ. Did that make sense?

Many people think that, just because a person is a Christian, it gives them the right to take advantage of them, including employees. Our mindset is that Christians are supposed to be full of love and skip-to-my-lou every time they walk. In the workplace, this is an opportunity to not do what they say and we think it gives us the right to run all over them. The Bible says differently. We should have 'Jesus work ethics'.

Love of Money
1 Timothy 6: 3-10

If I were to sit here and think of all of the cool things I wanted, I could probably make a list. It would start first with a big fancy house fully furnished with the latest décor for every room. I'd get a brand new Jeep colored red with custom black leather and off-road tires jacked up a few inches. You know, a bass boat would be nice and maybe get all new fishing stuff. I would take my kid's advice and upgrade my wardrobe a little and trade in my 1980's fashions for some of them modern duds that's popular these days. On the entertainment side, I would upgrade my VCR for one of them blue ray things and definitely get me the biggest flat screen TV they had at Wally World. You see, I wouldn't want much.

As a Christian, I know I am supposed to be content with the things that the Lord has blessed me with. My current Jeep and home is paid for. I have clothes. Even though they're out of style, they still serve the same purpose. If I look around me, I realize that I have everything I need. And that's awesome and I'm thankful.

I remember a few years ago when the economy was good, folks like me worked and were able to buy those things we wanted. As our demand for stuff increased, we would work more and harder to get the money to pay for it. I will admit that other things in our life had to suffer, like time spent with family. God and church stuff was one of the first things to be put on the back burner. It seemed material things were more important at the time.

But, all of a sudden out of nowhere, the economy crashed and the jobs were gone. Now we had more time on our hands than what we knew what to do with. For me, I did a lot of thinking and reevaluating the situation. To make a long story short, I realized that I and most of the folks in the world were materialistic. This 'chasing the American Dream' came with a price. The family had suffered because they had been neglected. We were spiritually malnourished because we had turned our backs on God in our pursuit for money. Problems were created because we weren't focused on the things that should have been important. It's the very same thing that Paul was telling Timothy about.

People back in the day were teaching false doctrines and neglected sharing the truth of Jesus Christ. Because of this, there was a lot of controversy and junk being said back and forth. Confusion was being created. So, why would this have even happened? Just like everything in the world today, it's all about the money.

You see, these false teachers probably realized they could draw more attention if they simply made up stuff. If they could draw a crowd and make them enjoy what they were saying, then at the end of the speech, they could drop the 'money ball'. You know, they could say stuff like:

"For a love offering of $19.95 in camel coins, you can get this cool shiny scroll with all of the same stuff you just heard. But wait! There's more! As an extra bonus, we'll send you these 'Walk Like A Disciple' sandals ab-so-lute-ly free!"

It then becomes about business. It's like any other profit-making company out there trying to sell you stuff. If you can make the crowd like you, they'll buy stuff from you. If you can make them feel good about themselves and their sinful nature, they will easily become a customer. You see? Cha-ching!

Paul was telling Timothy to stay true to Jesus and be content with the things he had; like clothes and food. From personal experience, it's easy to focus on all the stuff we don't have and to do everything we can to get it. Many times this involves neglecting the important stuff.

Paul's Charge to Timothy
1 Timothy 6: 11-21

Keep on keepin' on! That's what Paul would of said to Timothy if he were here today. Paul knew the pressures and the junk we face when we are trying to live the life that God wants us to live. Being a Christian is the easy part, but living it is a different story. Since we know that we are being molded to be like Jesus, and Jesus was perfect, we should quickly realize that a lot of work has to be done to get us there.

Paul was saying to flee from all the junk and to pursue the things from Jesus' example. Pursue means *to follow in an effort to overtake or capture.* The key word here is *'effort'*. We have to make an effort in following Jesus. Just like Timothy, we have to pursue:

Righteousness
Godliness
Faith
Love
Endurance
Gentleness

The benefit would be that, not only would we be better people, but God could use our life to lead others to Him. That's the cool part.

I love verse 17 because it hits home. We, globally, are currently living in bad economic times. It's all because of greed and that many of us put our trust in money for so long. Money decided a few years ago to let us down and we all fell hard.

As I am writing this book, many companies all over the world have been forced to close, the housing market is flooded with foreclosed homes that people couldn't afford, and the future ain't looking too bright.

We should of listened to Paul's warning.

The Book Of
2nd Timothy

The Book Of 2nd Timothy

Encouragement to Be Faithful
2 Timothy 1: 1-18 and 2: 1-13

Paul was thankful to God for everything in his life and he served Him with a clear conscience. It wasn't out of selfish ambition or for the money. He shared the same Christian faith that generations before him had.

It seemed he was always praying for this young fella named Timothy. He must have remembered the days before Timothy knew the Lord. He could have been your typical teenager; thinking he knew everything about life and how he wanted to live it. He probably thought he was in control and did everything that went against what others tried to tell him. He might have been a rebellious youth – a youth gone wild!

Paul looked back on the influences in Timothy's life and mentions the faith of his grandmother, Lois, and his mother, Eunice. It seems that because of them, they were part of Timothy's decision to follow the Lord. And another thing that is interesting to me is that Paul doesn't mention Timothy's father and grandfather. Could Timothy had been a fatherless child? Maybe a child whose father abandoned him at an early age? It's possible. Then, Paul would have been sent to Timothy from God to act as a 'fill-in' to give him the fatherly direction to make it in life. Keep in mind, the Bible doesn't specifically say this, but it is something to think about.

What would it matter anyway? Many kids these days grow up without Dads in their life and they turn out fine, right? It could be that the ones you see have had some Godly influence from a neighbor, a friend, or Christian family member. The ones you don't see are usually the ones in prison. There have been studies on behaviors of fatherless children and the statistics don't show positive results. In Timothy's case, Paul may have been used by God to rescue him. Maybe that's why Paul cared about him so much.

"To Timothy, my dearly beloved son..." - 2 Timothy 1: 2a

As Christians, we are strong because we have the power of God working in us and for us. Because of that, we should hold our heads up high, walk in strength and be brave. We don't have to be afraid of what the world can do or say to us.

What shall we then say to these things? If God be for us, who can

This gives us the courage to face any mountain and any obstacle 'head on' because God is working on our behalf for His glory. Everything we face has a purpose, no matter how scary it seems. It could be to make us stronger in our faith and/or to bring the Lord glory. God knows about the situation and is in control of it. We shouldn't fear.

These scriptures tell us that God doesn't give us the spirit of fear. This tells me that it comes from Satan. God gives us the spirit of power, love and sound mind. We should be living in peace knowing that God is in charge of our life. We should love one

another because having Him in our life creates this fruit in us to share with others. That's power, folks! It's the kind of power that affects lives around us. That's what it's all about.

Paul instructs Timothy to not be ashamed of the work he was doing or to let the idea of Paul being a prisoner get him down. He wanted Timothy to continue sharing the Gospel and telling folks about Jesus regardless of the suffering that was to be expected. Keep on keepin' on! The simple Gospel – God loves us, calls us and sent His Son to die for us. All we have to do is believe and take the offer – the free gift of eternal life. That's pretty simple!

Paul illustrates the stuff it takes to be a minister of the Gospel. He uses three scenarios: a soldier, an athlete, and a farmer to explain it because all three must be willing to make sacrifices.

A soldier gives up worldly security and endures discipline. An athlete must train hard and follow the rules. A farmer works extremely hard and is patient. If everybody keeps pressing on, we would glorify God, win souls for Jesus, and one day see Him face to face. That's the victory, the prize, and the harvest. That's good stuff, ain't it?

And remember, God will never turn his back on us. That's what I got from the last three verses. Did you?

A Workman Approved by God
2 Timothy 2: 14-26

Paul is telling Timothy about how to be an effective worker for the Lord. From the verses it seems that one of the tools we have is our mouth because of the stuff that comes out of it. It can build people up and lead them to the Lord. Or it can tear people down and confuse them and lead them astray.

It's important that we watch our words carefully. It's almost like we should think about what we are going to say first, and if it glorifies God or encourages others, let it flow. If not, we should probably keep our mouths shut. The reason here is that the

362

world is looking at us through magnifying glasses. If we're saying that we're Christians, people will try to find flaws in it to try and justify why they're not. We may be the only 'Jesus' they see and we should make sure we are representin'. You know?

If we are in a position of sharing God's Word with others, we have to be careful of how we present it. We shouldn't get into debates about Christianity, the Bible, God and all that stuff. This creates arguments and folks start getting mad. It doesn't solve anything. All we have to do is share the Word and let it do it's own thing.

The important thing, as Christians, is that we're serving the Lord. If we have junk in our life that is keeping us from being effective, we should throw it in the garbage. Turn from it! The Lord wants us to be vessels for Him to do some cool stuff. He wants to pour from an empty vessel that's clean, without that yucky residue from last week's leftover gunk. Would you want to drink from something like that? I wouldn't either.

Let's get rid of the sin in our life that's holding us back.

Godlessness in the Last Days
2 Timothy 3: 1-9

Keep in mind, this letter to Timothy was written by Paul back in A.D. 67. That's a long time ago! Almost 2000 years! Paul is talking about the last days. These are the remaining days before Jesus returns to get his people. From the sounds of what Paul is saying, there's going to be some moral decay going on. People are going to be changing in a negative way like Jekyll and Hyde. Here's a list of the changes to expect:

Lovers of themselves
Lovers of money
Boastful
Proud
Abusive
Disobedient to their parents
Ungrateful
Unholy
Without love
Unforgiving
Slanderous
Without self-control
Brutal
Not lovers of the good
Treacherous
Rash
Conceited
Lovers of pleasure rather than lovers of God – having a form of godliness but denying its power

We are told not to have anything to do with these kind of people. Maybe because their stink will rub off on us and we'll be acting the same way.

Paul mentions two names as an example: Jannes and Jambres. These were the Egyptian magicians that opposed Moses and Aaron from the Old Testament (Exodus 7: 10-12). They were able to do the same tricks and fool people. The same will be true in the last days.

There will be false teachers that claim to be the 'real deal', and just like magicians, they will 'trick' folks into following them and their wrong way of thinking. We need to be careful and compare notes. We need to study God's Word for ourselves so that we will know for sure.

Paul's Charge to Timothy
2 Timothy 3: 10-17 and 4: 1-8

Paul gives Timothy a warning that applies to us today, "Folks that want to live godly lives for Jesus WILL suffer persecutions." What would this mean?

That means if we decide today to start living 'souled out' for Jesus, we might as well gear up with armor. We should probably put some padding on and a bullet-proof vest. Having a helmet on wouldn't hurt either. The fact is we're going to go through a life of conflicts and people ain't gonna like this new you. The extremes of persecution could vary from 'name calling' to death threats. This is some serious stuff!

But, here's the deal. The choice to live this life comes with some awesome benefits like leading the lost to Jesus; souls being saved. Plus, you will have the Lord working with you during the rough times so you won't be alone. The key is to stay true and endure. It's too easy to just give up. Living the Christian life can be challenging but the price is worth it in the end.

Verse 16 is a powerful verse that explains the purpose of the Bible.

All scripture is given by inspiration of God, and is profitable for doctrine, for reproof, for correction, for instruction in righteousness: That the man of God may be perfect, throughly furnished unto all good works. - 2 Timothy 3: 16, 17

At the date of when this letter was written to Timothy, Paul was referring to the scriptures in the Old Testament. This was what they taught and studied from. The scriptures were helpful because they came directly from God to people inspired by Him to write down. It's Gods plan for godly living. So what about the New Testament? Is it included? Yes. These were inspired by God to different folks, too.

The purpose is to help believers live the life that God wants us to live. Everything we need for living is in there. We shouldn't study the Bible to just gain knowledge or use it as a tool to beat up on some non-Christians. We should apply it to our lives and do what it says. Our newly transformed life then becomes the example for the world to see. This life leads folks to Jesus.

And since we know that the Bible is God-inspired and 'God-breathed', we should get excited about reading it because we know it will be coming directly from Him. We shouldn't think of it as a book full of ancient stories that don't apply to us. It's through these stories and the experiences of the people it talks about, we can read God's love letter to us.

Here's another cool verse:

Preach the word; be instant in season, out of season; reprove, rebuke, exhort with all longsuffering and doctrine. For the time will come when they will not endure sound doctrine; but after their own lusts shall they heap to themselves teachers, having itching ears; And they shall turn away their ears from the truth, and shall be turned unto fables. - 2 Timothy 4: 2-4

Paul is talking to Timothy to be ready at all times to share the Word. This applies to us even though some of us aren't preachers behind the church pulpit. We should be ready at all times to proclaim what God's Word says to anybody at anytime. Like Paul says, there will come a time when people will not want to hear the truth. They will turn to false teachers that will preach messages that will make them feel all gooey inside and make them feel good about the sin they are living in.

We live in a day now where many people won't go to church or read the Bible. Some of these folks have turned to some teachings from hippie spiritualists or 'feel-good' preachers and think every thing is OK with their soul. We may be the only 'true' preaching they will hear. Every day becomes an opportunity to 'preach the Word'. This could be at the workplace, at a ball game, or on aisle 3 at Wall World. We have to be ready!

Personal Remarks & Final Greetings
2 Timothy 4: 9-22

These verses are sad to me because it seems that many of the people that Paul trusted in his ministry has deserted him. He was all alone and lonely. No one even showed up at his trial to speak on his behalf. Wow! Major let down!

To put this in today's world would be like if you were in charge of a powerful ministry. You and your team had seen lives change and things were happening. Well, all of a sudden, your ministry hits a brick wall. Maybe it was from some financial setbacks or hard times. This is when the strength of your ministry is tested. Every member is put to this test. This includes everyone from the speakers to the floor sweepers. The 'weakest links' bail out. The good thing is knowing

the Lord is still in control and can rebuild this ministry with the strong ones that remain. Sometimes I wonder if the Lord allows things to happen to see who will buckle under the pressure.

I believe this also applies to the home and not just ministries. If a family chooses to live for the Lord and follow Him, there will be situations that tests our strength and faithfulness. As a unit, our spouses and children are included in making up the home-based ministry. We should all stay rooted in the Lord and expect junk to come our way. If we're rooted as a family, we will be able to stand against the storms. The Lord will help us do it.

The Book Of
Titus

The Book Of Titus

Introduction To Titus - Who is Titus?

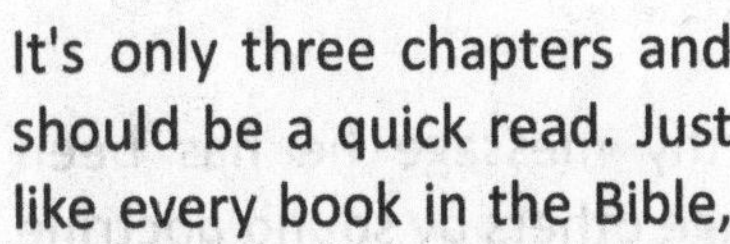

Titus was a Greek Christian fella that was probably converted through Paul's ministry. And just like most Greeks, he probably had dark hair, dark eyes and a big nose. But that's OK! He was on the team and served by being in charge of the churches on the island of Crete. The purpose of this letter from Paul to Titus was to help him do the job.

The Book of Titus was written probably around A.D. 64 from Macedonia while Paul was in prison. Paul wanted to give him some instructions on how to run the churches. It gives the responsibilities, qualifications of a pastor and how good folks should act in the world.

It's only three chapters and should be a quick read. Just like every book in the Bible, there will be some good stuff that we can apply to lives. Let's kick back and see how the Lord uses Titus and Paul to get His message across. Let's relax and soak it all in!

Titus's Task on Crete
Titus 1: 1-16

The purpose of Titus being in Crete was to finish the 'unfinished' business. His mission was to appoint elders in every town. That sounds like a simple job. All he would have to do is look for a bunch of old fellas with gray beards and give them a church membership badge, right? Wrong. There was more to it than that. An elder had to have certain qualifications to be able to fill the position. Here's the list:

He must:
1. be blameless.
2. be the husband of one wife.
3. be a man whose children who believe and aren't considered wild and disobedient.
4. not be overbearing.
5. not be quick tempered.
6. not be given to drunkeness.
7. not be violent.
8. not be pursuing dishonest gain.
9. be hospitable.
10. be one that loves what is good.
11. be self controlled.
12. be upright.
13. be holy.
14. be disciplined.
15. hold firmly to the trustworthy message he has been taught so that he can encourage others by sound doctrine and refute those who oppose it.

Was it possible for Titus to find good standing men to fill this position as an elder under these strict guidelines? I bet they were hard to find.

That raises another question. Are the people leading our churches today qualified based on these credentials? We may find that some churches don't use these guidelines at all. That would be a bad thing because the church wouldn't be effective in the community. Remember, this was God's plan for the church to help it to be a light in the world. Any slight modification or overlooked credential could mess things all up. As a church, we should make sure our leaders measure up to what God wants. You know?

Another job assignment given to Titus was to silence the rebellious people that were stirring up lies. Paul was mostly referring to the Judaizers. And no! I'm not talking about the sprinkly stuff you put on steak to tender it up and junk. These were the religious Jewish people and they were teaching stuff that wasn't true and destroying households for dishonest gain. Titus had to put them in their place.

The interesting thing to me was that these folks professed to know God, yet it didn't show in their actions. If a person truly loves God and is really living for Him, it will express itself outwards. People will notice the good fruit in the way they talk, act, and treat others.

How do others see us? If we are

375

claiming to be Christians, can we back it up with more than just words?

That's a little something to think about.

What Must Be Taught to Various Groups
Titus 2: 1-15

The interesting thing to me from the verses is that Paul is telling Titus to teach sound doctrine to a certain unlikely group of people in the church. By doing so, they can in turn, teach to others. This group of people being taught by Titus were the older generation (men and women) and the slaves. The lessons to be taught to the older men are to be:

1. Temperate
2. Worthy of respect
3. Self-controlled
4. Sound in faith, love, and endurance

And to the older women,:

1. They should be reverent in the way they live
2. Shouldn't be slanderers
3. Shouldn't be addicted to much wine
4. They should teach what is good

By teaching the older generation these things, they can train the younger generation:

1. To love their husbands and children
2. To be self-controlled and pure
3. To be busy at home
4. To be subject to their husbands

It's about passing down values from the older generations. Their families can learn from their experiences and avoid having to make some of the same mistakes they had made. Older people should be a role model (an example) to the younger generation.

The early church placed value on the 'seniors' back in the day. Sadly, some churches and society today overlook their importance and it could be the reason for the moral decay in values. It seems that kids have lost respect for their elders and will pay the price on down the line.
Think about this. If we had learned the values from our parents and grandparents of the 1950's, do you honestly think we would allow the garbage that's in the world of media today? By looking at the increase in crime, you'll see that there is a price for neglect. It will continue to get worse.

Paul also instructed Titus to teach the slaves to be subject to their masters in everything. He didn't want them to talk back to them or steal from them. Instead, they should build trusting relationships. The purpose is that this characteristic would lead people to Jesus.

This applies to us in the working world. The slave/master relationship is the same as the employee/boss relationship. As employees, we are setting the example in the workplace. Our actions reflect our characteristics as a Christian that our fellow workers and bosses will see in us. This will, in turn, direct them to Jesus.

It's cool how this all works.

Doing What Is Good
Titus 3: 1-15

One of the problems in society is that we have lost respect for our rulers and our authorities. We have this idea that all government people are dishonest and greedy, so we build this anarchy-type mentality. This may be true and their wrongdoing is between them and God. It doesn't mean we shouldn't still show them respect and not be subject to their authority over us.

378

It's Biblical.

There are several scriptures that tell us to respect our leaders. This includes Senators, Governors, and even our President. The thing we need to realize is that God is in charge of them and has put them in place. A country that goes against their government creates chaos and loses morals in society. This ain't good for everyone living in it.

Our authorities aren't just the people in the White House. It's also the people that are over us like our teachers, bosses, and parents. We should also show them respect and do what they tell us. It's the duty of Christians to do good in the eyes of the folks looking at us. It sets the example of a good citizen; a reflection of Jesus.

We are saved because of God's mercy on us, not because of all of the good things we have done. However, we do goods things because we are saved and the Holy Spirit lives within us. To devote our time to doing good things is a fruit of living for Him. The amazing thing is that it branches out and everyone benefits from your goodness.

That's productive living and it's pretty cool!

The Book Of
Philemon

The Book Of Philemon

Introduction To Philemon - Who Is Philemon?

To be honest, I nearly forgot all about this book from the Bible. It's another one of them small books that consists of one chapter with 25 verses. Plus, the tab thingy got flipped inward and made it hard for me to find.

Who was Philemon? He wasn't part of the original 12 disciples. It doesn't say anywhere in the Bible that he was a church leader or won any trophies for his awesomeness as an evangelistic super hero of the faith. All we know is that he was a friend of Paul and that he owned a slave named Onesimus.

Unlike the other letters in the Bible, this one was written by Paul back around A.D. 60 to Philemon as a private, personal letter to a friend. In today's world, it would be like a long email to a close buddy. The purpose of this letter was to convince Philemon to forgive his runaway slave and to accept him as a brother in Christ. I'm sure we will learn more about this as we read it. But, I'm guessing it's a letter about forgiveness and how we should treat others that have now become Christians — as our fellow brothers and sisters in Christ.

There's definitely gonna be a lesson or two in there for us. I guarantee it!

Let's check it out!

Paul's Appreciation of Philemon
Philemon 1: 1-7

Paul was in jail... again. This time, according to my Bible's footnotes, he was in house arrest. This gave him the freedom to continue his ministry because people could actually come and visit him. The Lord wasn't finished with him yet. Even though Paul was now old as dirt and sitting around writing letters all day, God still had a purpose for him. We know now that Paul was writing for what we call now, The New Testament. Isn't that amazing?

Sometimes I wonder what was going through Paul's mind back in the day. He was a changed man with a fire for the Lord. I'm sure he wanted to travel the world sharing the Gospel with anybody and everybody. But, instead it seemed like he spent more time in prison writing letters. I bet he felt like his time was being wasted, don'tchu? Paul did have a few moments where he would travel; building churches and sharing Jesus with folks. But, his important job may have been the God-inspired words he took the time to write. By doing this, generations after generations have been able to learn from him and lives have been changed along the way. That's cool to know.

This tells me that if God calls you to do something, regardless of the environment He has you in, you should do it. If we are called to preach or teach and we're sitting in an empty room with a pencil and a piece of paper, we should do it? How? Just write it down because that's the tools He's given us and we don't know where God wants to send that piece of paper. You know what I'm saying? That's how I feel today in my ministry. All I have is a laptop

with a flickering screen, a Bible, and a job duty. No audience! I have to be obedient and put the rest in His hands.

Paul begins by thanking Philemon for who he was in Christ and for the love that he had for folks. It brought joy and encouragement to everyone. It seemed that God used him to keep folks pumped up in the faith.

Have you ever had a bad day? As Christians, we are going to have times when we are feeling down. It's normal. Isn't cool how that special someone will come into our life, maybe through a phone call, and will say something that sorta turns things around for us? That person is a blessing because they encouraged us. God used them for that one special purpose that we needed right then and there. Weren't we thankful? It made all the difference in the world to us, didn't it?

That's how Paul is feeling and he is speaking to Philemon on behalf of all the others that were blessed by him. They were refreshed! Sorta like drinking a Mountain Doo on a hot summer day!

We should be a blessing to others like this. The world has enough negativity floating around. We should ask God to help us to become a 'positive' in someone else's life out there. It might change the world.

Paul's Appeal for Onesimus
Philemon 1: 8-25

Beginning in verse 8, Paul is requesting something from Philemon. Based on Paul's authority as an elder and leader, he could have just bossed Philemon around by making a few demands. But, Paul wanted him to do something and he asked him out of love. What was it that Paul wanted him to do? Let me tell you the whole story first.

According to what I've learned, Onesimus was a runaway slave. That would mean that Philemon was a slave owner and his slave decided one day to just take off. Back in those days, if a slave did something like that, the slave owner had the right to kill them. A slave was treated more as a possession than as a real person.

But something cool happened. Onesimus met up with Paul in prison. This was probably a low point in Onesimus' life. Paul led him to Jesus and he was saved. His life was changed and was now a Christian.

Philemon, who was also a Christian, had to accept Onesimus as a fellow brother in the Lord and not as a possession. He would have to see this man now as an equal and forgive him of his wrong against him. This would be the Christian thing to do and would be kinda tough.

Paul was sending Onesimus back to Philemon. Paul was willing to take full responsibility for him. He said he would pay the price for any of the wrong that was done in his past. This must have been a serious deal hearing Paul say this. This would let him know quick that Onesimus was a changed man since Paul was on his side. I'm sure Philemon trusted Paul's judgment.

The lessons here are about forgiveness and acceptance. As Christians, we have to forgive folks that have wronged us. The same price Jesus paid for us to be saved and to be forgiven, He paid for everyone. This includes that person we find it hard to forgive. We gotta let it go!

Then came Peter to him, and said, Lord, how oft shall my brother sin against me, and I forgive him? till seven times? Jesus saith unto him, I say not unto thee, Until seven times: but, Until seventy times seven. - Matthew 18: 21, 22

Also, if a person is a Christian, we have to forgive them of their past and not use it against them. They are a new creature in the Lord. We should accept them as our brothers or sisters and quit holding their past over their heads.

And when ye stand praying, forgive, if ye have ought against any: that your Father also which is in heaven may forgive you your trespasses. But if ye do not forgive, neither will your Father which is in heaven forgive your trespasses. - Mark 11: 25, 26

Forgiveness is a major step in finding the peace that Jesus wants us to have. If you decide not to forgive, it will only build up bitterness, resentment, and pain. You won't be able to move forward in your Christian walk. You don't want that to happen, do you?

The Lord wants us to live life and live it abundantly. He can give that to us today. If you don't have it, you may want to ask Him to save you. A simple prayer that's sincere from the heart is all it takes.

If you're a Christian, it could be that you're holding a grudge against someone that you need to forgive. It could be a relative, a friend, or that fella that cut you off on the expressway today. You know, the one that made you say all those ugly words and extended your middle finger. Let go of that junk that's holding you back. Take the steps you need to take today and get it all squared up.

I want to live, don'tchu? A'ight then.

More From A BackPew Review

Thanks for reading this guide. We hope you enjoyed it and will continue to read our other guides in the series. Here is a complete list of our books from the series:

- **What Does It Mean To Be A Christian**
- **Acts: The Early Days Of The Christian Church**
- **Being A Dad According To The Bible**
- **The Prison Letters: Apostle Paul's Letters To The Early Church**
- **Exodus: The Journey To The Promised Land**
- **Genesis: The Beginning, The Fall And The Promise**
- **The Seven Letters: The New Testament Letters To The Early Church**
- **The Gospel From A Four-Sided View**
- **Healthy Eating: A Few Tips From The Bible**
- **Being A Man According To The Bible**
- **A Marriage Built To Last: Learn What The Bible Says About Marriage**
- **How Do I Pray? The Bible Tells Us How**
- **Revelation: The End Is Near?**